What Others ~~~ ~~~~~~~

"Powerful. Inspiring. Personal. Vulnerable. I began reading *Save the Butter Tubs* on a recent flight, and I was so captivated by each page that I did not want the flight to end. Brenda has the unique ability to communicate as a writer and speaker through personal life stories. She helps you focus on your God-given potential rather than the many distracting limitations we face in life."

Alex Velarde, Lead Pastor, LifePoint Fellowship Church, Tyler, Texas

"Only someone like Brenda could have written *Save the Butter Tubs*. She knows from experience how light can shine from the broken places of our soul. You will never think of a butter tub the same way again if you grasp the message of worthiness Brenda shares through her writing and speaking engagements."

Joan L. Turley, author of *Sacred Work in Secular Places*

"In *Save the Butter Tubs*, Brenda shares the five lies that hold us back from our biggest dreams. She reveals—through her journey and her grandmother's—how you already have all you need to live the life you want and leave a legacy that matters."

Kary Oberbrunner, author of *Your Secret Name, The Deeper Path,* and *Day Job to Dream Job*

"Brenda Haire is a vibrant, passionate woman of God who is a gifted writer and speaker. Her book, *Save the Butter Tubs*, shares a powerful message of realization that we are enough and have enough to leave an indispensable legacy. I cannot wait to see how God uses her, and His message through her, to change thousands of lives."

Andrea Fehr, author of *Freaking Out to Flying Free* and founder of Flying Free Ministries

"Brenda Haire is living the portrait Jesus painted when He shared about 'coming so that we might experience life to the full.' *Save the Butter Tubs* was birthed through the transformation that comes from discovering that God does not want us to live *for* Him—He desires for us to live *from* Him! WARNING: Don't pick this book up thinking you'll read a little here and there. Once you start, your heart will be drawn to this personal journey and God's desire to write the next chapter through your life as He has mine."

Ken Hicks, Lead Pastor, Heights Community Church, San Antonio, Texas

"Sometimes the overall complexities of life have an uncanny way of hindering the maturity of our spiritual and even our psychological well-beings. Having attended a small group ministry, in which Brenda Haire was the leader/facilitator, I can say with honesty that Brenda will encourage and challenge you in her new book, *Save the Butter Tubs*, to rise above who you think you are and instead step into your God-created purpose. So, 'save the butter tubs'—because God doesn't make any throwaways."

Keith Lough, Pastor, King of Glory, Dallas, Texas

"I was sitting in church yesterday, and some of the words Brenda said in her book were resonating in my heart, and it just hit me . . . I'm not just procrastinating writing MY story, but it's HIS story. Because my life is HIS testimony. And people need to hear it! Not because of me, but because of HIM!"

Melanie S.

Save the Butter Tubs!

Discover Your Worth in a Disposable World

Save the Butter Tubs!

Discover Your Worth in a Disposable World

BRENDA A. HAIRE

Paperback ISBN: 978-1-64085-345-4
Hardback ISBN: 978-1-64085-346-1
Ebook ISBN: 978-1-64085-347-8
Library of Congress Control Number: 2018907491

Grandma, without your faith in me, I wouldn't know what it means to be fully alive. I pray this honors you and leaves the legacy you hoped it would.

Contents

Foreword

Does anybody even read a foreword anymore? If not, I'll keep it short and sweet so you can get on to the meat and potatoes. I met Brenda at *my* book signing for *Eat Cake. Be Brave.* She drove an hour and a half from her small town to my lovely Lufkin, Texas, just to meet me. She might be on to something with this brave thing.

Even though I had experienced my own tattooing of hurtful words throughout my life, I still cringed hearing what some publisher had the gall to tell Brenda. We live in a world where, before we can even begin, we must prove we are worth beginning. I'm done with that! I'm done proving my worth. I'm done with limiting belief. So is Brenda! Cheers to the overcomers!

No matter how empty or rejected you may feel, your tub is still valuable! The fullness of your tub doesn't determine your worth (literally and figuratively)!

Brenda is right about discovering our worth in this disposable world. When you know your worth, you will live accordingly. Everyone around you will benefit. So don't put this book down until you're transformed by the truth printed on these pages. Allow Brenda's stories and those of her grandmother to penetrate your soul. Because guess what? WE are the butter tubs! (Perhaps this is why my mom has saved every single one she has ever used. I'll have to tell her I'm sorry for making fun of her the past forty years.) And it is never too late to be who you were meant to be . . . I'm living proof of that.

So start now.

Turn the page.

Melissa Radke
Author of *Eat Cake. Be Brave.*

Repurposed Passion

"Anyone who thinks fallen leaves are dead has never watched them dancing on a windy day."

~ Shira Tamir

As children, my sister Jenifer and I spent our long Texas summers with my grandparents while our parents worked. My earliest memories include their single-wide trailer home. In its late 1970's décor, I thought it was fancy. Maybe it was the way Grandma kept house. Everything was in order and polished until it shined. Beds were always made. A doll with a wavy, pink, crocheted ballgown sat on the pillows in the guest room where we slept.

Jenifer and I played pretend at the bar off the kitchen. We would climb onto the swivel barrel barstools and play "office" mostly. I recall their brown Rolodex. I realize if you're younger than I am, you probably don't know what a Rolodex is. This is a desktop index where names and phone numbers were stored before modern technology. Grandma referred to it as her address book. They came in all different styles; one being cards on a wheel that you rolled over to flip to the contact you were looking for, hence the name "roll-o-dex."

Grandma's Rolodex was cool. It was the laptop of their time. It was a thin, rectangular-shaped tin case. The alphabet displayed along one side with a little silver arrow you would slide to the letter that corresponded to the name you needed. With the push of a button at the bottom, it would pop open like a jack-in-the-box to the card inside correlating to the letter you selected. I'm surprised we didn't wear it out! I found it when we were cleaning up her estate. It still works over forty years later!

That's the thing about my grandparents, they rarely parted with things or bought new things. I only recall them having two living room sets my whole life. They didn't see the need to buy things just to have them or to replace things that didn't need replacing. Wow, what a concept! Sadly, not many Americans live with that mentality today. I have the utmost respect for how Grandma lived her life.

While staying with Grandma during a visit home to San Antonio, I received the greatest gift she could have ever given me—she asked me to write this book. As it turns out, this would also be one of the most significant challenges and responsibilities of my life.

I first felt called to write in 2003. I had a scare with a lump in my breast. While stepping off the elevator at the mammogram facility, I ran into an old colleague. Theresa and I had worked together in the hospitality industry years before. She was someone I admired. Her work ethic, drive, and approach were like no other colleague I had worked with. She was now in pharmaceutical sales, and I was in direct sales. We exchanged business cards while speaking briefly. She announced she was writing a book and would soon be leaving her job to pursue her dream career. I thought, "Wow, she has a dream, *doesn't she?*"

Don't get me wrong. She was certainly capable of accomplishing her goal, but my lack of dream-ability couldn't see it. I had never known anyone who had written a book. I didn't know the first thing about it. It was just one of those moments I questioned: "Why, after all these years, would I have run into her? Why now?"

Desperately searching for reason in my life, I picked up a copy of *The Purpose Driven Life* by Rick Warren[1]. I thought, "Here is the one book that will solve this dilemma once and for all." I couldn't read it fast enough. I wanted the answer. I wanted to understand how my life and all that I had experienced mattered. I was so tempted to skip to the end to see if the answer was there in plain sight.

I was about halfway through the book when I received a postcard in the mail about a book signing. I couldn't believe it! Theresa's dream was coming true. She'd done it! She had published her book. Witnessing this opened my mind to a whole new level of opportunities. I had to go to the signing. I had to get a copy of her dream!

My husband, Darren, and I drove to the small bookstore in the middle of San Antonio. When we arrived, Theresa was talking with customers while signing books. I was amazed. "Wow, she did it!" She not only wrote a book, but she also accomplished what she said she would. Something that I couldn't see—she saw it. She had a vision, and it came to pass. The best part for me was yet to come.

It was my turn for her to sign a copy of her book, appropriately titled, *70 Secrets to Self-Discovery*[2]. I didn't even know what to do. I had never been to a book signing. Was I supposed to pay for the book first or have her sign it first? The clerk directed me. While she was signing, I asked her what her plans were. She shared how she was presenting a workshop called "I Hate My Job." I told her I didn't have a job to hate but was looking to find one that I could love. She urged me to come to her next workshop, and I quickly agreed.

It was a dark and stormy night—it actually was—and it turned out I was the only one who showed up for the workshop. God and His perfect plan, I'm sure! Theresa presented her materials, uncovering lifelong dreams I had buried years before—buried under so much pain and bitterness, I couldn't see them, much less reach them. Our time together wasn't a counseling session but a workshop full of hope and discovery. It was forward-thinking.

Continuing to read *The Purpose Driven Life*, God confirmed in my heart what Theresa and I had uncovered at the workshop. "Your greatest life messages and your most effective ministry will come out of your deepest hurts. The things you're most embarrassed about, most ashamed of, and most reluctant to share are the very tools God can use most powerfully to heal others."[3]

Theresa began to coach me in the direction of my dream, and I started working on business plans. I would stay up all night working, writing, and putting it all together. Full of passion for my newfound purpose, I was ready to make it happen. I recall telling Darren, through my happy tears, that I finally felt like I understood what God wanted me to do with my life. I realized why every rotten thing had happened to me and how God was going to use them for good.

God saw this book before I had ever dreamed of it. Sometimes your greatest gifts come out of necessity. I didn't create it—I was *given* it. God knew. "'For I know the plans I have for you,' says the LORD. 'They are plans for good and not for disaster, to give you a future and a hope.'"[4]

In 2009, I took a couple of journalism courses and published some articles in the college newspaper. I sent the newspapers home to Grandma, my mom, and sister Jenifer. Grandma was an avid newspaper reader, and Jenifer still is. Mom, well, she doesn't read the paper, but I just wanted her to be proud. She was but quickly pointed out a mistake that was missed by five editors and myself! Yikes! In the story I wrote, my subject received a bone marrow transplant *after* her death, according to the dates! Either way, Grandma must have been impressed because this book is a result of those articles.

Clockwise from left: Mom, Grandma, Me and Jenifer

During my visits home, I always started my day chatting with Grandma over her first cup of coffee. I'd fetch the morning paper, and we'd discuss how she slept. This particular morning, as I sat down, I could tell something was different about her. She was giddy. Bursting with excitement, she reported that she woke in the middle of the night, sat straight up in her bed, and received a revelation from God that I was to write a book about all the good in her life.

"Here," she exclaimed, "I've already started!" She handed me a tattered notebook, in which she'd jotted down some thoughts: "A memory of one person's pilgrimage (footsteps) through life; memories of my journey of a very full life." As I read those words, I felt honored and humbled—as if I was touching a piece of precious history. I was holding in my hand the beginning of this book, the beginning of a journey with my grandmother down memory lane—*her* memory lane—one I hadn't gone down too often.

Oprah Winfrey is a polar celebrity. People either love her or hate her. I don't know how you feel about her, but I'm sure you can agree with this quote: ". . . every single person you will ever meet shares a common desire. They want to know: 'Do you see me? Do you hear me? Does what I say mean anything to you?'" We want to know if we matter. We want to know if our life is adding up to anything meaningful. I believe this is part of the reason Grandma asked me to write this book.

I don't recall Grandma being much of a storyteller before this. Most of my memories were about her teaching Jenifer and me how to "put a little elbow grease into it." She taught us how to work hard and to be ladies. Oh, what I would do for another summer cleaning her house just to hear her say that one more time. Back then, we felt we were the reason child labor laws were enacted: we cleaned windows with newspaper and vinegar, polished table legs, and took down every curtain in the house to be washed, dried, ironed, and rehung. It seemed like we awoke with the game show *The Price Is Right* and went to bed after *Wheel of Fortune*. I don't know what time those shows came on back then, but that was our schedule. Grandma was a stern woman. We used to call her Sergeant Grandma behind her back.

Reflecting now, I'm thankful for each lesson she taught us. I understand even more now why she kept things so neat, and what a great way that is to keep a child busy! Grandma respected and valued her possessions, home, and life. As you will read, Grandma grew up without indoor plumbing, air conditioning, or running water. Oh my, how times have changed. The house she lived in when we started this book journey must have felt like a mansion to her. Her modest four-bedroom/three-bath home wasn't at the top of today's market, but it was her little piece of the pie.

What started with Grandma sharing some great memories has turned into a book of valuable lessons on how to live a "full life," as Grandma put it. She has left a legacy that will live on through those she's impacted. Like a ripple, her legacy will continue to reach farther than she ever thought, thanks to you. My prayer is that you will begin to trash the lies holding you back, treasure the truths, and transform your life into a fulfilling journey—leaving a legacy of love.

As you read, I hope you enjoy the excerpts in italics. These are the unedited stories or direct quotes from Grandma, unless otherwise noted. She hand-wrote her stories in a tattered old notebook. I can't tell you how much I treasure these writings. To learn how to collect writings from your loved ones, visit my website at brendahaire.com.

The last time Grandma and I spoke about this book, she advised, "Be clear and sincere." She wanted to make sure the message was understood. I invite you now to listen to the heart of one of the most magnificent women I ever have had the honor of learning from and from the broken heart of someone that misses her beyond belief—me.

Sometimes your greatest gifts come out of necessity.
#WorthSaving

PART 1

Trash

CHAPTER 1

Lies We Eat

"A life of distractions will never produce a life of meaning."

~ Kary Oberbrunner

I announced on YouTube that I was the "Queen of Creative Avoidance." Of course, this was after I had creatively avoided starting a YouTube channel for months! Just days into my vlogging (video blogging or logging) journey, I announced I was going to clean out my closet and asked for some tips. The next day, I found myself creatively avoiding cleaning out my closet. I needed to start Christmas shopping. After all, I was in town running errands, so I figured I might as well make the most of it. The truth was, I didn't want to clean my closet. Not that I didn't want a clean closet, I just didn't want to be the one to do it. Thankfully, I had challenged myself publicly and figured the world would hold me accountable.

Most people think of arts and crafts when thinking about creativity. You might not consider yourself a creative person, but the truth is, we're all more creative than we realize, and this chapter will be very telling. It will identify how you creatively avoid your potential by numbing it. Creative avoidance comes in many forms.

When I finally stepped foot into my closet after creatively avoiding it all day, I realized my list of reasons for avoiding this task was longer than just not liking to clean.

1. It was a reminder that I wasn't in the shape I wanted to be. Not everything was my current size.

2. Some of the items were reminders of jobs, experiences, and days gone by. Some I missed, some I didn't want to remember.

3. I'm not an expert in organizing and don't like to clean.

4. I'm not a fashionista or stylist.

5. I bought some of the things in my closet while creatively avoiding something else.

6. I seriously don't like the latest clothing styles and can't seem to find my style.

7. Would this attempt at cleaning and organizing my closet last?

Wow, I sound like a big whiny baby. What a bunch of first-world pettiness! After realizing why I'd creatively avoided this task for so long, I took a deep breath and asked myself a question: *Is the way my closet looks right now serving my mission?*

You see, I decided to take off my "Creative Avoidance Crown" and take back the crown God placed on my head when He forgave me. He paid for that crown in full. I'm a child of God, and since He is the King of Kings, that makes me His princess. I'll gladly wear that crown, knowing that I can do all things through Him who strengthens me. My excuses do not limit what God can do. The Holy Spirit opens our eyes to see the everyday miracles that surround us, the ordinary miracles that are us.

My mission in life is to help people move through their faith journey. No matter where someone starts, there is always room for growth. My passion is to help others see their potential, know their worth, and act accordingly. It greatly saddens me to see so many people merely existing when they already have all they need to thrive fully. Knowing your mission is going to be the first step in changing your crown. After many, many years of creatively avoiding my purpose, I'm now finding clarity with each step I take in faith. If we don't take a step forward, we will always be in the same place.

No matter where your faith lies, I'm sure of this: deep down you're yearning for something bigger. The problem is that we don't know how to get to the goal, so we creatively avoid it altogether.

Here are the most common creative avoidances:

Drugs

Alcohol

Food

Shopping

Sex

TV

Busyness

Changing jobs

Over-educating

Hobbies

Socializing

Napping

Most of these things aren't bad. In fact, I'd go as far as to say they're all good in moderation. Yes, even drugs. You need certain medications if you're sick or in pain. But when they become obsessive, addictive, or used to avoid your mission, they become a problem. Look around and you'll see that people find ways to creatively avoid what they should be doing or even what they desire to be doing. If you're honest, this may be you right now. We distract ourselves with something that temporarily makes us feel good and is socially acceptable.

After God placed the dream in my heart to write, I started learning as much as I could about writing and publishing. I even took some of my first manuscripts to a writers conference. I received great feedback from the publishers, but they insisted that I was a "nobody" and to come back when I was a "somebody." That left me hurt and confused. I continued studying about writing and the industry. I never stopped journaling my thoughts or capturing stories.

When Grandma asked me to write her story, a fresh excitement stirred. I began gathering information during my visits with her, but when it came time to put those thoughts in order, I put it off. I didn't know what I was doing. Occasionally, I would work on the project, outlining and organizing Grandma's notes into categories that then became chapters. In no time, I found myself stumped again. Not sure how to proceed, I just didn't. In the meantime, Jenifer encouraged me with gifts and trips to historical family landmarks. I would commit to writing, but then, nothing would come.

I found my greatest fulfillment while writing, but I couldn't see how a "nobody" was going to make a career out of what was—at that point—a hobby at best. I mean, if I were to become a writer, I would have to write, right? Instead of writing, I was taking other jobs. Ultimately, I decided to go back to college a second time, thinking that I would create a better plan, a safer strategy than being a broke, vulnerable writer. I wanted to avoid that sad stereotype! My new safe plan was to become a high school communications teacher, hoping that would provide fulfillment. After all, I would be pursuing two things I love: teaching and communicating. The first semester was great! With a 4.0, I was off to a good start. By the second semester, I was beginning to wonder if this was going to be enough for me. I was student teaching and felt confined. I loved educating and inspiring students, but each day the walls would close in a bit more.

Spring break of 2016 was a game-changer. Darren and I have been hiking in the woods for over ten years, and never do I recall being bitten by anything, much less a tick. Somehow, after a visit home to San Antonio, I suddenly found myself sicker than I'd ever been. It started with a small bite mark on my leg that looked unusually red. It grew over the course of a week until it was larger than the palm of my hand.

Being silly, I took a picture of what looked like a bullseye and posted it on Facebook, calling it my "burning ring of fire," even though it didn't burn. A nurse friend of mine recommended that I go to the emergency room to get checked for Lyme disease. That was Saturday morning. I was feeling a bit run down but not bad enough to go to the ER. I had no idea what Lyme disease was or that a bullseye rash was an indicator. By Sunday evening, disabling dizziness left me in bed. On Monday, I couldn't function, and a trip to the ER was in order.

The emergency room doctor confirmed it was Lyme disease. He prescribed ten days' worth of antibiotics. It was late evening when he called the prescription into my small-town pharmacy. I asked him how soon I needed to start taking it. With certainty in his voice, he declared, "Right away!" I told him that my pharmacy closed in two minutes and asked if he could call it into a chain pharmacy that was open later so that we could pick it up on the way home. He did. We picked up the ten pills of hope, and I took the first one as directed.

I quickly learned as much as I could about the disease because now I had it, and it was debilitating. Everything spun. I couldn't even watch people talk, as their body movement made me nauseous. No television or social media—every little thing moved way too fast. I was weak and afraid that like many Lyme patients, I would have it forever. I researched and talked to anyone I could about it. I heard about only two people that had acute Lyme disease and found a cure within a reasonable amount of time: one person within six months and another within the first thirty days. I prayed for the thirty-day treatment!

Lyme disease is very controversial and hard to treat. At the time of this writing, there are two Lyme disease specialists in the state of Texas, and they aren't in my area. Lyme disease is a bacterium that gets into your bloodstream through an insect bite and then multiplies continuously. The entire lifecycle of the bacteria needs to be killed to rid yourself completely of it.

With so few doctors familiar with Lyme disease in Texas, I would've had to travel a minimum of two hours, one way, for further treatment. I read story after story of patients suffering for years with Lyme disease. I was afraid I'd be facing months of traveling for treatments and—worse—months of suffering. A woman at the university I was attending at the time told me that her sister had been suffering for over twenty years. I was terrified! Praying was all I could do. I was sick and in the fight of my life. I felt God had a plan for me and that this wasn't it. I asked God why He had stopped me in my tracks. I was busy pursuing this safe new career and then, boom! My world was literally spinning upside down. I felt like God was trying to get my attention.

As I tossed and turned in bed all day, wondering if I would ever get better, I went round and round with God. I kept praying, asking Him what I should do. I begged Him to heal me. I bargained with Him. I told Him I would be obedient to anything He asked if I could, please, get out of that bed. He just kept saying to me, "I've already told you what to do, and you're not listening. I told you to write. You're pursuing the wrong things. Your faith is wavering. You either trust me or you don't."

It seemed like this was our daily conversation—not that God was speaking out loud to me, but to my spirit. It had been thirteen years since I first felt called to write. I felt like God was saying, "Enough already! Do I have your attention now?"

Initially, the ER doctor gave me only ten days' worth of the antibiotics. I was able to get another eleven days' worth by calling my doctor and quoting the Center for Disease Control's (CDC) guidelines[5] and recommendations for twenty-one days of treatment. In the back of my mind, I was convinced I needed at least thirty days' worth of treatment. I had no idea how I would get the nine more pills for the thirty-day cure I was after.

About day seventeen into my treatment, I asked Darren to pick up another medication I take regularly. When he came home and handed it to me, I was pleasantly surprised! It was ten more days of the antibiotic I needed! God worked it all out. Remember that prescription called into my small-town pharmacy? The doctor never canceled it. God must have had His hand in this because my pharmacy has a policy of restocking anything left over seven days. That prescription had been there for seventeen days!

I didn't start feeling better until about day twenty-six or twenty-seven. After all the stories of people suffering for years, I knew I'd received a miracle! Now it was time to move forward. I began to pick up where I left off back in college and student teaching. I felt obligated to finish what I had started, but God reminded me that He didn't bring me to my knees to remain the same. He was trying to get my attention, and I needed to be obedient.

I was slow to respond because of the commitment and investment I had made in going back to school. I thought I would take an incomplete grade for the spring semester and make up the work over the summer, but, in my spirit, I felt I was still hanging on to my backup plan.

Ultimately, I responded by "burning the boats" and moving in the direction I felt God wanted me to. If you're not familiar with the idea of burning the boats, it famously comes from Hernán Cortés, the first victorious Spanish conqueror of Mexico in 1519.[6] Cortés ordered his men to burn the ships in which they had arrived, leaving them no choice but to fight or die. There was no retreating.

For me, burning the boats meant dropping out of college. Getting a degree was a big deal to me. I was a good student. In a mock interview I had for a teaching position, the interviewer said she would hire me on the spot if she could. Getting a job was never the issue; getting the *right* job was. I finally decided I either trusted God or I didn't. I burned the boats. I would fight for my dream of being an author or die trying.

I believe that I'm going to heaven because Jesus died for my sins, so why couldn't I trust God with this? It was time to sit and write. That is the only way the book gets from my heart to yours. Unfortunately, that was not the magic moment of "Ta-da, here's the book!" Many distractions still snuck their way in between me and my laptop. To be honest, I've allowed many things to get in my way—grief being one of them.

Jenifer called Sunday, January 29, 2017, just three days after my birthday, with the horrible news that Grandma had fallen and broken her hip. She was in the hospital and would require surgery. I packed up and headed to San Antonio, not knowing if I'd get there before they took her into the operating room.

Guilt for procrastinating so long on this book was torturing me on the five-hour drive south. Even though Grandma was ninety-three years old, I always thought she'd hold a finished copy in her hands. That's a delusional thought when your actions aren't aligning with your dreams. What made me feel she would outlive my creative avoidance? Grief overwhelmed me.

I made it to the hospital before her surgery. I was able to hear her say my name one last time. She was loopy with all the pain medications. Over the next couple of days, surgery proved to be too much for her kidneys, and her body began shutting down. When you see the most influential person you've ever known at their weakest, there are no words. It was heartbreaking.

I'm so thankful that I was able to be there with Jenifer. During the last night in the hospital, we had what Jenifer refers to as "one last slumber party with Grandma." We both stayed the night, curled up in uncomfortable, plastic chairs in her hospital room. We listened to Grandma breathing and shared stories and secrets that only sisters can understand. It was bittersweet.

The next morning, February 4, 2017, Grandma passed away with my hand on her chest as she took her final breath. I was devastated. My creative avoidance had outlived Grandma. She passed peacefully with family by her side. I stayed an extra day to help Jenifer with the arrangements before traveling back home to get clothes and the rest of my family. Together, Jenifer and I crafted the obituary. How do you honor ninety-three years in three inches of print space?

After submitting the obituary to the local paper, Jenifer received a call asking for additional information. A reporter wanted to interview us for a featured article about Grandma. Jenifer called me and suggested that I should do it since I was writing this book. We agreed that we both would be on the call. We were nervous but excited as the reporter asked question after question. We both shed tears but were left with an awe-inspiring joy. It meant so much to us that they were honoring Grandma in this way.

We told the reporter about Grandma's more than thirty years in the catering business, as well as her humble, yet inspirational, beginnings. We held a lovely service for her on Valentine's Day. It was appropriate, for she was truly one of our greatest loves. My daughter, Beth, and daughter-in-law (or daughter-in-love, as we say), Rachel, sang "How Great Thou Art" at the graveside portion of the services. It was beautiful.

I often wonder if that reporter will ever realize the impact of that call. It was such a gift. Jenifer and I needed that. Grandma deserved it. It pushed me to buckle down and get this book finished. Creative avoidance has finally taken a backseat to necessity. Editing Grandma's story into past tense and writing about her final days were painful, but the lessons her life has taught me can't be contained in me. The title of this book comes from Grandma's habit of saving empty butter tubs and jars. There was always a pile on her counter to usher home leftovers, pot a houseplant, or hold odds and ends. It epitomizes the story of Grandma's life. She saw the potential in people, experiences, and things. Everything has a purpose and value beyond what we see on the surface. Lessons fill moments, people are packed with potential, and things have multiple uses.

Since Grandma's passing, God made it clear to me that *I* was the "butter tub" that she saved. Just as she saw the unused potential in an empty butter tub, she saw the untapped potential in me. She saw me as a vessel that could carry her story forward. She believed in me. Jenifer believed in me. It was time I started to believe in myself and the plan God has for me. Digging deep, I asked myself why I had creatively avoided writing for so long. The reasons sounded eerily familiar to the reasons I avoided cleaning my closet. They may be some of the same reasons why *you're* avoiding what you're meant to be doing: insecurity, perceived lack of knowledge, the past, or fear of repeating failure. They're all the same underlying reasons we avoid so much of what is waiting for us.

The wait is over. If you're going to creatively avoid what you're meant to do for a day longer, do it by finishing this book. I know your worth. My prayer is that you realize it for yourself. Your purpose is more magnificent than napping or binging on anything. "Both addict and artist are dealing with the same material, which is the pain of being human and the struggle against self-sabotage."[7] Stop avoiding your potential. Stop sabotaging yourself. Whatever you're called to do is more significant than any mess you've created to distract yourself from acting on it.

Stop avoiding your potential.
#WorthSaving

CHAPTER 2

Lies We Believe

"Those who wait for perfect weather will never plant seeds; those who look at every cloud will never harvest crops."

~ Ecclesiastes 11:4

I've never considered myself a control freak. Control is an illusion. I'm not an overly obsessive person. Change doesn't bother me the way it does other people. I like the adventure of it. I don't need a plan—just a loose outline. I'm fully aware things can change in a heartbeat. That awareness came the hard way. Several times in my life, I thought I was in control. I felt confident in the direction my life was heading and the plans I had made. Suddenly, circumstances changed, and I realized I wasn't in control. In 2016 when I decided to go back to school, Lyme disease put the brakes on. God was reminding me that He was in control.

Even with this book, I tried to control how much of God and scripture I would include. Grandma wasn't boisterous about her faith. I wanted to make sure I honored her, but how could I question leaving Him out when the entire story is about Him and how He works in our lives? I had to ask myself, who is my reader? What is the purpose? Remember that Rick Warren quote: "Your greatest life messages and your most effective ministry will come out of your deepest hurts. The things you're most embarrassed about, most ashamed of, and most reluctant to share are the very tools God can use most powerfully to heal others."[8] The truth is, I didn't feel qualified. I don't have a theology degree. Who am I to write about God and quote scripture? I'm His. And He says, "Now go and write down these words. Write them in a book. They will stand until the end of time as a witness."[9]

That's all He wants from me—my story. I'm not perfect, but God is. He can use me and my mess as a ministry that will reach others and move them along their faith journey. When I started to write freely all my thoughts and stories about how God was working in my life, this book went from nine chapters to fifteen overnight. I was writing from my circumstances, not trying to create a story that reads better than real life. Life is messy. We can't control everything that happens to us and around us, but we can control how we respond.

Jesus tells us, "And you will know the truth, and the truth will set you free." So I could continue to skirt the truth, or I could write it. It's not that I was being deceitful, I just wasn't being authentic. My dream of helping people move along their faith journey had to come out. If it died within me, a part of me would die. I can't afford that. I need to be fully alive.

It was even more difficult because I was including Grandma's story. In wrestling with the direction of this book, God spoke to my heart: "I was there all along." He was right. Grandma shared how her faith carried her through her circumstances. She believed God would work things out. I've always had the same faith, so now it was time to act on it.

God will work out the details and outcome for this book. We can't control the outcome. There is very little we *can* control. We think we can control our children, our environment, our health, and so much more. The truth is, we can influence all of these things, but we *can't* control them. People think they can control their health, but some things we have to manage, not control. For instance, I have a gene mutation known as Factor V Leiden. It basically means I have sticky blood cells, and I'm more prone to clotting. I can't change that. I was born with it. It's genetic. I can influence it with blood thinners, diet, and such, but I can't change it.

It's disturbing to see people trying so hard to create the illusion of perfection. They are trying to control the perception of others. "Too many people spend money they haven't earned, to buy things they don't want, to impress people they don't like."[10] I'm sure you've met someone like this—maybe you are someone like this. You want every detail of your life to seem perfect to the outside world. You dress a certain way, maybe you buy name-brand things you can't afford, to appear to be in a particular income bracket or fit in with the supposed elite. People find security in what we believe they have. So many times people are trying to control one area of their life because another area has gone completely bonkers. Control is often used to mask pain or to give you a sense of security. You overcompensate in one area of your life because you feel helpless in another.

The problem is that we're too busy trying to pursue what isn't ours to pursue, including God's work. We need to do what we were created to do and allow God to work through us. We take matters into our own hands and end up in a puddle of pity when it doesn't work out. You need to decide—either you're god or He is.

If we trust Him for our eternity, we should be trusting Him with our lives on earth. But we're too busy trying to be like someone else or live someone else's dream. We let the world tell us what we should be doing, what we should have, how we should look, and what actions we should take. Then, we immediately feel like failures because we drifted out of our lane.

We're not supposed to be what the world tells us. We're to be who we were created to be. You *are* a unique gift to the world. That's your superpower! "It's hard to lead a cavalry charge if you think you look funny on a horse."[11] It doesn't matter what you think you look like. If you were called to do it, *do it!* Stop trying to control what others think about you. Like the saying goes, "You'd care less about what others think about you if you realized how seldom they do."

The worst part is not that we worry what others think, it's that we change our behavior based on what we think they believe. One of my favorite authors, Steven Pressfield, wrote this: "When we can't stand the fear, the shame, and self-reproach that we feel, we obliterate it with an addiction." Confidence is silent; doubts are loud. We judge our insecurities in others. What we say about others, exposes more about us. We tell ourselves, "I'm not good enough" or "I have to become *this* or *that* to fulfill my purpose." These lies take us away from our truth. Caring what others think is a control issue. When we start comparing, we're letting our egos control us. Let passion control you. Passion comes from the soul. It comes from deep within.

I consider myself to be generous. I volunteer several times a week, give to charities, help out friends, and forgive people reasonably quick. Back when the book I was writing was a very different book—before Grandma asked me to write her story—I wrote this in my journal:

> After a much-needed refreshing night sleep, I awoke an hour and a half earlier than my alarm. Thankful for the rest, I felt like God wanted me to spend the extra time with Him. Meditating and singing to myself, I knew

this time was set aside for God but didn't know how He would have me use it. The weight of this book was heavy on my heart. It wasn't going to write itself. My thoughts brought me back to the purpose and what I still had to lose to live on purpose. Maybe I should write the book in two sections—fear and doubt. These common obstacles keep us from God's will for our lives. Fear and uncertainty lead to overeating, depression, a desire to control things that are out of our control, and isolation, but what it comes down to is disobedience.

I decided I would get up and write. I knew God had something to say. It was time to get things in motion. I started the morning by reading a devotional and was blessed that God had a new message for me. Many times my devotionals confirm what God is telling me in other areas, but this morning it was fresh. The lesson: selfishness.

I felt convicted that my feelings about being obedient were all about me. If I were obedient, my life would be full and abundant, as God promises in His Word. I would finally be called an author, fulfilling what I believe is my purpose. It was all about me. The devotion talked about how we could be the sweet fragrance that reminds God of Jesus' life on earth. If you have a sense of smell, you know a scent can take you back in time. The smell of baby shampoo or lotion always reminds me of my children when they were babies. I can even feel their sweet skin and recall what it was like to hold them in my arms. Now wrap your mind around the fact that we can cause God to have memories of a sweet time, a time when He was living as a man on this earth, a time when He was redeeming the world. God reminded me that He is a feeling God. The Bible tells us not to grieve the Holy Spirit.

For so long, I focused on how God offers mercy and grace and how my works don't get me into heaven. It's only by His grace. Therefore, I turned works into something for me and about me. I felt like the only person affected by my obedience or disobedience was me. While I understand my obedience would point to God and be about His will, I didn't consider His feelings. How selfish would it be if a friend asks you to do something, then after a long hesitation you finally agree, but you procrastinate, never doing what they asked and never once considering their feelings? How long would that friendship last?

We're blessed that our God is patient. He uses the time we waste for His good by teaching us valuable lessons along the way. Is your selfishness keeping you from God or His purpose for you? Are we putting our own selfish desires above His? How much time are we setting aside each week for God—giving ourselves freely and unselfishly, to just be pleasing to Him and not getting caught up in the outcome for us? Time isn't a renewable resource. How we spend it should be a priority.

There are 168 hours in a week. If we're blessed enough to sleep eight hours a night, we spend fifty-six hours a week sleeping. If we work full-time, we spend at least forty hours at work and, let's just say, an hour a day commuting, so there's another five. If we exercise an hour a day and go to church on Sunday, that's another seven. This leaves us with sixty hours. Give yourself an hour each morning to get dressed and an hour each evening to fix dinner and enjoy it. Now we're down to forty-six hours. How are you spending those forty-six hours each week? Driving the kids to extracurricular activities? Grocery shopping? Housework? Homework?

Divide that time out over the week, and we have an average of over six hours a day. Everyone's schedules are different. I have more time because my kids are grown, and I currently don't have a traditional work week. Trust me, I hear about my flexible schedule all the time as a writer. "Since you don't work . . . blah, blah, blah . . ." Fill in the blank. Let's settle this once and for all! While my schedule may be more flexible, my workload is no lighter. No matter how you look at your schedule, I want you to do just that—look at it. Sit down for a moment and write a list of the things you do on a regular basis. Do you see where your time goes? I can hear you saying, "God commanded me to rest, so I'm resting." How much rest do you need? You should be getting adequate sleep at eight hours a night and then resting on the seventh day. For some that could be Sunday. For others who work different schedules it could be another day. Just don't fool yourself into resting too much or not enough. Don't call laziness rest, trying to justify it. If you're using your time selfishly, you need to ask yourself why. Are fear and doubt driving you to be selfish? How are you impacting those around you if you're being selfish? What will your legacy look like if all you think about is yourself, your time, or what you want?

When you learn how to surrender to God and trust the plans He has for you, there's freedom like you've never experienced before. You'll start to screen your decisions through your purpose. You'll find it easier to say no to the things that don't align with your purpose. If buying those new shoes or new car isn't in alignment, you can walk away with confidence. That is a new control. You're now controlling your obedience. You're choosing to make decisions that will have eternal consequences.

You will begin to see the world through God's eyes instead of trying to be a god. Control what you can and allow God to work out the rest. The list of things you can control is substantially shorter than what you can't control. The kind of control we should be most concerned with is self-control. Self-control comes through surrender to the Holy Spirit in your life. Two things you can control that will have an eternal impact—your obedience and your attitude.

Have you ever had a prayer need but were too embarrassed to share it? I have. Not only was I embarrassed, but I was afraid people would know the other parties involved in my dilemma and talk about it with them. I fretted for about a year over a major decision and never once asked for prayer because I was too ashamed of the circumstances. Finally, one day when I was praying about it, a scripture came to mind, "Then if my people who are called by my name will humble themselves and pray and seek my face and turn from their wicked ways, I will hear from heaven and will forgive their sins and restore their land."[12] I did just that. I humbled myself in full surrender. I prayed, asking the Holy Spirit to guide those praying for my circumstances. I couldn't control what they did or didn't do with the information I was asking them to pray for, but I could surrender it. That was on a Friday. He answered my prayer on Tuesday. Imagine the stress I could have avoided if I was willing to humble myself a year earlier.

Humility is not a sign of weakness. Humility is a sign of wisdom. When you're humble, you know Who is in control, and you're willing to surrender fully. The grandest lesson God has taught me regarding authority is that if I don't understand Who is in control, He will gladly show me. I pray that you can learn this lesson from me and save yourself some of the trials that came with my power trips. If you find God pulling the plug on your plans, lean into Him. Those will be some of the sweetest times with Him, and the greatest testimonies will come from your surrender.

Two things you can control—your obedience
and your attitude.
#WorthSaving

CHAPTER 3

Lies We Buy

"Aspire not to have more but to be more."

~ Anonymous

My grandparents lived in only three houses after their trailer home. They moved from their single-wide, two-bedroom trailer home to a multilevel, three-bedroom home on a beautiful piece of property in the Texas hill country we called University Hills. The new house was spacious. It had a beautiful kitchen that opened on both ends—one end to the formal dining room and one to the breakfast area that overlooked a large living room. Up a half-flight of stairs were three bedrooms and two bathrooms. Jenifer and I had a guest bedroom with twin beds that flanked the window. We also had a new office space with a unique drop-leaf secretary desk in our room. It has little mail slots, and we would play at that desk for hours when we had time off from chores. I say "has" because I was blessed with it after my grandmother passed. It's one of the many treasured pieces of furniture I inherited. Not because it's expensive, but because of the memories it holds.

University Hills summer home

*Me in the driveway at Grandma's. I have no idea
why I'm holding my beheaded fish!*

Grandma and Grandpa's room was large and connected to their master bathroom and walk-in closet. In today's market, having an en-suite would be expected, but back in the late 1970s, early 1980s, it was like a mansion. There was an additional guest bedroom that had a full-size bed and a long dresser. Grandma kept her costume jewelry and scarf collection in there. Scarves were slowly going out of style then. They've made a comeback a few times since but always different fabrics and shapes. Grandma had an extensive collection, especially of sheer ones. I would tie one around my waist and then link or slip all the others through, making a skirt. I'm sure this is when I fell in love with tutus. They were so colorful and fluffy. Something about them felt forbidden. I'm not sure if it was because they were sheer or because we would sneak in to play with them.

Down a level from the living room were the laundry room and garage. The laundry room was small by modern standards, but considering my parents' washer and dryer were in our garage, having an actual laundry room seemed luxurious to me. We didn't go down there much except to carry the laundry—curtains and bedding mostly. The garage was off limits because that was where Grandpa stored his fishing gear, and we weren't allowed to play with it. Grandma was always warning us about the fishing hooks. Grandpa kept them neatly in a tackle box, so they weren't an issue. The only hooks exposed were the ones still attached to the fishing poles that leaned against the wall.

There was a small park across the street from the house with concrete picnic tables and benches. Jenifer and I would escape from our work days at Grandma's by hanging out in the park. Grandma also allowed us to walk through the neighborhood to the ice house on the corner of the highway. For those not familiar with the term "ice house," it's another name for a gas station. Before many of them sold gas, they just sold sundries and ice. Not the small pieces you buy in the bag to fill your cooler for the lake, but big blocks you would put in your refrigerator to keep your food cold. Ice houses existed before electric refrigerators or all of the fancy refrigerators we have now that make ice for us! I guess the term "ice house" was passed down from Grandma; I still call gas stations ice houses.

The house in University Hills was my summer home. My Christmas and spring break home too. The house reminds me of my innocence. Jenifer and I played with our Hot Wheels (yes, I think my dad wanted boys) along the fireplace hearth in the summer and warmed up to it in the winter. This house is where I learned of my parents' divorce when I was nine years old. While that was a heartbreaking time in my life, this home felt safe. Grandma shared, not only her home with us, but her heart. No matter which house she lived in, it was her heart you felt when you entered. She always welcomed, served, and loved.

Grandma lived a simple life. Simple doesn't mean boring. It means peaceful. It means focused. I often wonder if that contributed to her longevity. Living a focused life helped her financially to save and wisely invest. More importantly, it helped her leave a legacy that will live on for generations.

On more than one occasion when I was visiting Grandma, I would leave the house after our morning chats. She would always ask where I was going. If shopping was on the agenda, she would question, "For what? What could you possibly need?" One time she remarked that I shopped the last time I was in town, as if shopping every three to four months was too much. Now that I'm clear about my mission in life, I can say Grandma was right. What could I possibly need? Groceries are a different story, but even Grandma's snacks were simple. She recalled that as a child, she enjoyed cheese crackers. I'll always remember her enjoying oatmeal cookies.

Grandma knew her mission in life was serving others through her God-given talent. She loved people through cooking and entertaining—both in her home and along her career path. Her possessions supported her goals and dreams. Her focus allowed her to live an uncluttered life. God had already given her what she needed to succeed.

Do you find yourself in a cluttered space, mind, or life? External clutter is internal clutter on display. Is what you're filling your life with aligning with your mission? Does it align with your truth? Yes, your truth—the values by which you live, or, at least, the values by which you *wish* you lived. What someone treasures is often directly related to what they value.

Often the tools we need to accomplish our goals and dreams are right in front of us, but we bury them. Once we uncover the truth about what we need, we understand that we already have all we need to accomplish what is before us. Many times, we say we value something, but our actions speak otherwise. We create the idea of who we want to be in our minds, but it's clear we don't value the idea because our actions aren't in alignment.

For example, many people claim they value their health. However, they may never define what that means. Do they mean eating healthy? Going to the doctor on a regular basis? Exercising? Or any combination of the mix? What about the people who say they want to be authentic, yet everything about them is fake? Many women fall into this trap. Their desire is to be treasured and accepted for who they are, yet they're covering up with fake nails, fake hair color, fake tans, plastic surgery, clothes they can't afford, and the list goes on and on. They say they want to be fully known, but they're hiding behind too much stuff. Or are they seeking acceptance? If the whole world was blind, how many people would you impress?

Values + Action = Character

What we value and how we act on those values define who we are. Our character is how we show up in the world. If my values and my actions are aligned, I show up as a person of good character. If my values and my actions are out of whack, then I might appear shady. Sometimes we get good at putting up a front, but our soul pays for the damage of a shady character. We become an imposter in our own life. We desire to act a certain way, accomplish particular goals, and stand up for our beliefs; however, our actions let us down. There is a bigger picture we can't see with our eyes, but we feel it with our souls. You know that longing, that desire. Even if you can't put your finger on it, your soul knows there is more.

Once we fraud ourselves enough, we stop trying. We don't share our values or stand up for our beliefs. That, my friend, can be a slippery slope. A slick slide right into depression or addiction.

My pastor at the time of this writing takes this a step further, saying:

"Values + Action = Culture"[13]

It's incredible to me that we all consider ourselves to be individuals, but we become more like the people we associate with every day. We let others influence us in a way that doesn't necessarily align with our values. As a parent, I've told my children more than once that you become like the people you hang around the most. I've also watched as their friends have influenced them in ways that didn't align with what they claimed they valued. Television, media, and even the fashion industry play a huge role in creating culture.

As a child, I played in my mother's and grandmother's high heels. I certainly never owned any. Today, they are making wedges and two-inch heels for children! Slowly, we're sexualizing our children because that is what is available to the masses. The values of some affect the actions of others, and it can change a culture. I've struggled with swimsuits, as well. I want my daughters to be conservative but still stylish. Those two ideas don't go together in the fashion industry—primarily, in the juniors department. It certainly makes it hard to take a stand.

There's excellent news! Values work both ways. When we take a stand, we can create a movement. It starts with us. We influence our circle. Then the ripple effect continues. The emergence of the Tiny House Movement couldn't have affirmed Grandma's lifestyle more to me. Not that her house was small, but it wasn't excessively furnished or crammed with knickknacks. Everything served a purpose.

After returning from my first trip to the Smoky Mountains with Darren in 2006, I remember distinctly thinking I wanted to live a simpler life with fewer possessions and more experiences. We stayed for a week. The first three nights were in a studio-type room at a resort. Then we moved to a motel overlooking a stream. Both rooms were modest with minimal decorations. For a week, we lived it up with only one suitcase. When we returned home, I started wondering why I had all the things I did. Life was more straightforward with less stuff. Having fewer knickknacks means less to dust. A smaller space is just less to clean. Having a minimal wardrobe means fewer choices you have to make and less laundry you have to do.

There are two different movements right now teaching people how to shrink their wardrobes. The Uniform Movement is when you buy one outfit you love multiple times, and it becomes your daily uniform. Think Simon Cowell—he wears jeans and a basic white or black T-shirt every day. The Capsule Wardrobe Movement, my favorite, is building a smart wardrobe with coordinating items. You might base it on ten pieces that mix and match to give you thirty outfits. My current style is more of a combination of the two movements. Getting dressed is so much easier when you open your closet to see the clothes you know you can wear, and they all easily mix and match.

You may have never considered downsizing. You may find comfort in a space filled with the things you love. The question is, do you love them? Are they supporting your mission or hindering you? If you're ready to be free, ask yourself, do I love it? Does it bring me joy? Do I use it on a regular basis? If not, it may be time to pass it along to someone who needs it more than you do. Living with less allows for experiencing more.

If you need resources for downsizing, I suggest Pinterest. If you're not familiar with Pinterest, I probably should apologize for either your loss or for your new obsession. Just be careful not to get sucked into the idea of organizing your excess. Everything should have its place, but if you have too much, it may be time to part with the surplus. Remember, if it doesn't align with your mission, it needs to go! When I cleaned out my closet the last time, my qualifier was if I could wear the item to church the next day. We attend a church where anything from dresses, jeans, or long shorts are acceptable. I didn't include my workout or hiking clothes in the decision, but those weren't the clothes overflowing from my closet. For those items, I asked myself, *If I were going on a trip tomorrow, which of these items would I pack?* It was the best closet clean-out I'd ever done!

I love Pinterest because it allowed me to declutter my house of magazines. It has become my online magazine. Grandma always had a magazine subscription. *Better Homes and Gardens* was one of her favorites. She wouldn't hoard them, though; she passed them on to other people or recycled them. I loved getting copies from her and paging through the ideas. But then what do you do with them? Pinterest allows you to enjoy browsing pins of any topic. Then you can save them to a "board" to reference later. I have boards with recipes, capsule wardrobe ideas, and so much more. All of which can be easily shared.

Technology is moving quickly and has changed the way we do so much. As a writer and avid reader, I still have a bookshelf full of books. I reference many of them, but I've learned to let go of the ones that are no longer serving me. Grandma's estate consisted of mostly books, cookbooks, and recipes—as opposed to clothes or knickknacks.

Her wardrobe was pretty minimal. In her bedroom closet hung her everyday clothes. In another bedroom, there was a "museum" closet that housed the clothes she wore before she retired. Every piece was in excellent condition, and I was surprised at how sparse it was—maybe fifteen outfits. Jenifer; my daughter-in-love, Rachel; my daughter, Beth; and I went through the closets. For Jenifer and I, it was a trip down memory lane because we could recall Grandma wearing these suits and dresses. As we pulled each piece out, we could name the events she attended while wearing them. These were Grandma's favorites. She loved them, and she wore them confidently. There was no excess, no bulging closets—just a simple wardrobe that fit her mission.

For many years, I thought the way Grandma saved and valued things was because of the Great Depression. After visiting with her about this book, I learned that because her family had a dairy farm and grew their own food, they had all that they needed. She saved and valued things because there wasn't an abundance of options. She shared with me that many things were reused or repurposed.

It sounds cliché, but living was simpler in Grandma's time. There wasn't a big-box store on every corner with an abundance of choices for every perceived need. Instead of playrooms for their children, kids were entertained on the farm. Of course, by "entertained" I mean occupied with chores. It was rare for a homestead to have air conditioning. It was no big deal to spend your days outside in the heat, working with your hands and tending to the animals.

Grandma Recalls
Cultivating—Planting—Irrigating—Harvesting

*The things we learned about growing vegetables—
never a dull time. Spring and summer were always busy
planting and harvesting. Mother loved planting crops
harvested above ground. Tomatoes, green baby lima
beans, peppers, chili peppers, okra, roasting ear corn,
squash, and, of course, a few flowers for the delight
of all. Each crop had a different problem. Okra—you
wore a long-sleeved shirt, or the plant would sting you.
Sometimes, we also wore gloves. Corn—if the wind
was blowing, you also wore a long-sleeved shirt and
hat, for the stalks were sharp and would cut you. Chili
peppers—you soon learned not to touch your eyes until
you washed your hands.*

*We picked green baby limas and spent hours popping
the pods, which had two or more beans. We would put
them in a crock to carry to market the next morning to
sell by the pound. Squash was a backbreaking job because
the vines grew along the ground, and the squash grew
under the vine. How could I forget cabbage? We made
sauerkraut in crocks. Tomatoes had to be picked several
times a week with care, for the plants were brittle and
could break. Then came the canning season. We were
lucky to have a pressure canner, making it faster and
easier—good old mason jars. In the fall, we butchered
a calf and a pig. There were many ways to preserve the
meat—smoking some, some cured with salt, and some
put in large crocks covered with grease and stored in a
cool place.*

*At one time I recall my cousins living in a small
town south of us. Their parents had a grocery store.
Once a month, we went there for household staples. With
twelve dollars, we would get a twenty-five pound bag*

of flour, a large can of baking powder, a sack of salt, a five-pound bag of sugar, a large bar of Crystal White Laundry Soap, two bars of Ivory soap, and one pound of coffee for Mom. When many things were rationed during World War II, we often bartered with our cousins. We would bring our vegetables to the store in exchange for the things we needed.

When I asked Grandma about a special gift her mother gave her, she replied, "She gave me a dress pattern and yellow feed sacks to make a dress. I made a nice dress. I loved not having to wear hand-me-downs from my cousins."

Remember, we had many things we grew or made. Milk, cream, butter, cheese—we ground our corn into meal—eggs, chickens, bacon, meats, vegetables . . . nothing was ever wasted. I am amazed at all the waste. Landfills filled. When I was young, all things seemed to be used again and again in some way.

This conversation from the movie *The Book of Eli* sounds like a conversation Grandma and I once had:

"Tell me about the world before. What was it like?"
"We didn't even know what was precious. We threw away things that people would kill for today."[14]

It's not just that we're throwing things away that still have value, we're hoarding so much that others could be using. Maybe you've seen the show *Hoarders*[15], and you're saying, "I'm not that bad." Perhaps you aren't. I hope you're not because it's a sad and dangerous way to live. I am, however, willing to bet that you have excess stuff in a closet, pantry, attic, or shed. You are possibly paying for a storage unit somewhere. A new self-storage facility just went up down the road from us. It's unsettling to think of the amount of stuff our society hoards. Why on earth are we hanging on to all this excess when there are so many people in need? The reality is, those "valuables" you're hanging on to *just in case* you need them, you probably won't be able to find them when the need arises. I know, I'm guilty! If you can't find it, you might as well not own it.

Everywhere we look we're being enticed to buy something to make us feel better and look younger, or be smarter, stronger, and sexier. The underlying message is that *we're* not enough the way we are and that we need something external to make us better. The solution to this epidemic is simple, yet profound: understand your purpose and you'll understand your needs.

It makes sense to me now why Grandma questioned my need for shopping each time I visited. Sadly, I don't recall anything I bought on those trips. I'm pleased to say I'm letting go of the excess I've held dear for far too long. It's freeing. It feels like a weight lifted. It's easier to focus on my mission.

Simplicity was part of Grandma's secret to happiness. She only had one shelf of knickknacks. Most were gifts she'd received or souvenirs from traveling. The key to simplicity is this: know how you're gifted and how you will use that gift to serve others. That, my friend, is your mission. Once you know that, keep what serves your purpose. Keep what fills you, not what fills your space.

One item Grandma kept from her childhood was a statue of the Blessed Mother encased in a wooden box with a glass front. It was given to her when she made her First Communion when she was seven years old. My mother now has it. When Grandma knew we were clearing out her house after she moved to assisted living, she wanted to make sure we were cautious in transporting the statue to my mother. She asked several times if it arrived safely. You could tell it was something meaningful to her. It was the one thing she'd kept since childhood. The key being ONE thing! There was nothing in Grandma's attic, no shed to clean out, and no storage unit. Her estate consisted of dishes; cookbooks, along with recipes she loved and used for entertaining; furnishings she'd had for decades; the two closets of clothes I mentioned earlier; and an office full of paperwork. (I'm sure she just didn't know how to dispose of it properly to protect her identity.)

I'm thankful I have many pieces of those furnishings now. It was hard deciding what to keep. We have a modest house, fully decorated, with little room for more. I selected pieces that had meaning to me and that I knew I had a place for in my home. I didn't want anything ending up in storage, and I'm trying to simplify, remember?

One of the hardest decisions, at the time, was what to do with Grandma's oval dining table. It took me a while to decide if I was going to keep it. Jenifer and I discussed it for months before cleaning out Grandma's house. We went back and forth, trying to find a home for the beloved table that held so many memories. As children, Jenifer and I would crawl under it to polish the pedestal as part of our dusting chore. I can remember pretending to be a waitress, serving the adults as they played poker around its large, slick, oval top. They would tip us a quarter now and then. I learned to set a formal table complete with water glasses, bread plates, and dessert forks at this table. Subsequently, Grandma taught my daughter how to do the same.

We passed the turkey, giblet gravy, relish tray, green bean casserole, mashed potatoes, and Grandma's famous dressing (or stuffing, depending on where you're from, I guess) around that table. I still prefer to put a meal on the table and pass the dishes around or pass plates. Something about serving each other in this way seems like the way it should be. It was always fun to see if we could fit all the food on the table amidst the formal place settings and condiments. We always had too much food because Grandma cooked as if she were catering to the President and his motorcade. Hence, the butter tubs—there was always a stack on the counter, along with empty jars. We would fill them with leftovers, and everyone would take home meals for the week. Recycling was a way of life for Grandma long before recycling was cool.

A few months into the great table debate, I made a decision. You see, I teach a group in our home on Wednesday nights. As we squished around my rectangular table, with corners jabbing into the unfortunate ones who straddled the legs in those spots, I stood up, took a picture, and texted it to Jenifer. "I'll take the table!" We entertained at that table three times within the first week of having it. I'd never before put it together that I love to entertain as much as Grandma did. It's indescribable how entertaining at her table fills my heart.

I can still remember clearly the last time I sat across Grandma's table with her pool-blue eyes looking back at me. We were having breakfast tacos. My favorite is refried beans, cheese, and bacon. Grandma preferred just bacon with egg. Interestingly enough, I've found that different parts of the country—and even in Texas—people don't know what a breakfast taco is. If you're reading this and have no idea what I'm talking about, you have to try some of these South Texas staples. Tortillas are for sopping up a sauce and cradling delicious ingredients, from beef and vegetable strips, which we call fajitas, to eggs with bacon, and anything in between. Tortillas are like bread but flat and round. Tacos can be served any time of the day, depending on the ingredients.

I don't recall the kind of taco I had that last breakfast with Grandma, only the conversation. I wish I could go back in time and have fewer tacos and more conversations. My hips wish that too! Grandma would ask about my life back home, and I'd do my best to paint her a clear picture. The best way I can describe my small town is that it's like San Antonio was when I was a child. It's slower. There's less traffic, fewer people, and less hustle and bustle. That was part of the appeal when we moved here. We wanted to slow down and enjoy life. It seems now I'm watching this small town race to catch what we left behind in San Antonio.

No matter where you live, slow down and ask yourself if the stuff you're surrounding yourself with is causing you stress or bringing you joy? What do you need in life? Trade out the store-bought junk for the family heirlooms, display the vacation pictures, and savor the moments that matter. In the end, you can't take your physical belongings with you. When your loved ones sort through your estate, what will your belongings say about what was important to you?

As a whole, we've created idols out of anything and everything—entertainment, food, work, and so much more. Good things intended for pleasure have become idols. We even have a reality television show called *American Idol*[16], providing more options for us to focus on something else besides God. Now, I can hear the argument in your mind: "It's my downtime. It relaxes me. It's entertaining." That may very well be true, but the question is, do you spend more time focused on God or these distractions? It's time to focus on your mission. What excess is keeping you from your full potential? What is burying you?

Our sin is the darkness that is trying to hide our light. It's our lampshade. Don't let excess in any form shut out the voice of God. Don't allow excess to become your lampshade.

Life is short. Don't buy the shoes. Buy a friend lunch instead. Life is about relationships, not stuff. Stop filling your life with things. Stuff doesn't fix our broken hearts. It doesn't fill us with the hope we need to survive. Dig deeper. It's not about the material things. It's bigger than what we can see. Our circle doesn't need more of our stuff; they have plenty of their own. They need more of *us*. Focus on making memories and deepening relationships. "A rise in prosperity is not making people happier or healthier; create space for God's Kingdom to break through."[17] If given a chance, the enemy will persuade you to exchange the worship of the Creator for the worship of the created. Let creation be a reminder of the characteristics of our Creator and direct your worship back to Him. Stuff makes an awful god!

The only thing you need can't be taken away from you.
#WorthSaving

CHAPTER 4

Lies We Tell

"I attribute my success to this: I never gave or took an excuse."

~ Florence Nightingale

If anyone could have had an excuse not to succeed, Grandma could have. She had an eighth-grade education, graduating at age thirteen with only two other girls in her class. She grew up on a farm with few of the amenities we enjoy and often take for granted.

My dad dug many wells trying to get water, but it was not fit for use because it was sulfurous. The smell was awful. We collected rain runoff from the roof of the house and the barn into a metal cistern, and we brought water back from town in the same ten-gallon cans we used to deliver milk to the creamery. Daily, Dad took our milk, my grandpa's, and my two uncles', to the creamery close to where Brackenridge Park is now. Once in a while, I was allowed to go with him. I remember the streetcar and hearing the clanking of the trolly bell. I don't know where it started from, but the end of the track was on South Flores Street, out by St. Leo's Church.

J.J. Appelt delivering milk from the dairy and picking up supplies for the general store

Dad built a generator for us to have electricity until Rural Elect brought in lines on overhead poles. There was no sewage system. We had an outhouse built over a hole in the ground. We would move it when it was necessary. There was no such thing as trash service. There was a small amount of trash, for nothing was wasted. There seemed to be a use for things. Items were reusable. The small amount left was burned in a large barrel or buried.

I would like to tell of the house I grew up in, a very modern home except for the plumbing. It was built about two years before I was born. From a small front porch, doors entered the living room. A side door entered a large room with lots of windows. We often used it as a bedroom in the summer so we could open all the windows. A small interior room was commonly used as a bedroom in the winter because it housed the wood stove. We used a smaller room as a bathroom. All that was in there was a cabinet with a large pitcher and a wash bowl. We bathed in a large washtub with water carried back from town. In the kitchen, we used water collected in a cistern. The kitchen had a large wood cook stove, a family table with chairs, and a bench along one side. There were some cabinets for dishes and a pantry.

Later, my dad built another room on the side of the house that became our country store. Eventually, he buried tanks for gasoline. The pumps had a transparent glass cylinder on top. When someone ordered a gallon, you'd pull a manual handle back and forth to pump the gas out of the underground tank into the cylinder, which measured the gallons. From there the gas was dispensed by gravity, down the hose into the car.

The circus came to town and used the side of our store to advertise. They gave us tickets to the show in exchange. Some of my days were spent helping in the store. Once, when I was about eight years old, I was tending the store when a tough gal and guy asked for the restroom. I told them it was an outhouse in back. The lady insisted I take her there while the guy drew the gas. They paid for a couple of gallons. I always felt they filled up, but I was too scared to confront them. I'd never seen them before and never saw them again. If we saw a wagon of gypsies pull up to the store, my sister Josephine and I were told to hide, for the gypsies were known to steal blonde little girls.

Sound like a crazy tale? When I was in college history class, my professor told the same gypsy tale! I've never cared much for history class, but that day, that class came alive. I knew the stories my professor told were true because, five hours south, Grandma was sharing the same stories!

When I was nine years old, my dad died at home after having a kidney operation at age forty-six. They thought no one could live with only one kidney, so they cleaned his calcified kidney. He only lived three months after surgery. His brother stayed with him until he passed. He was then taken to the Angelus Funeral home, for his friend Mr. Guerra owned it. Dad was embalmed and brought home for an all-night vigil. My mother stayed up while the children slept. He was then transported by hearse to San Francisco de la Espada Church for Mass, with burial to follow at San Fernando Cemetery.

Dad was buried in a lined wooden box that we purchased from the funeral home. Some families of the Mission couldn't afford to embalm their loved ones, so they were buried the next day. Some families made the coffins for their loved ones and transported them on a flatbed truck or wagon.

Julius Joseph Appelt

Grandma's childhood was far from playrooms, video games, and over-the-top birthday celebrations. She never had a bicycle or learned to ride one. Her childhood games were, as she described, "Tug-O-War, Hop Scotch, and soft-baseball, if we could find a ball. The bases could be anything. Bats were sometimes available, if not we used a broomstick." There were no televisions in people's homes, no Saturday morning cartoons like I watched as a child—just chores.

We spent our Saturdays getting ready for Sunday: washing my hair, ironing clothes for church for the family and me, killing chickens and plucking them, readying vegetables, and baking bread for Sunday dinner. As for Sundays, we all went to church and had a lovely meal after.

Grandma said she never pretended to be sick as an excuse to stay home from school because "it was easier at school than staying home."

I was twelve when I learned to drive, for Mother did not drive. I had been operating the tractor and truck on the farm. When I was sixteen, I drove into town to take the milk to the creamery. My brother served in the United States Army in World War II, which left me with many responsibilities. I was the only one left to drive and farm with the tractor. WWII was a changing time for everyone. Women took over jobs in factories where needed. We all pitched in and did what we could. We rationed things, but no one complained. We just helped each other.

Grandma was twenty-one years old, working at Mr. Wong's Grocery, the first time she used a telephone. Phones have come a long way. There was no phone on the farm. At the time of this writing, we have smartphones that never leave our sides, take pictures, allow us to video chat with anyone around the world, and act as our calendar, calculator, alarm clock, and more. Mr. Wong's phone looked much different. Grandma recalled it was a box hanging on the wall with an earpiece attached to a cord. You spoke into the box. There was no dial; you turned a crank on the side of the box to ring for the operator to help you connect the call. This type of phone is known as a wall crank telephone.

Of Her Time at Mr. Wong's Grocery

We taught each other. Working on the farm helped me learn how to package many things. One of the older owners was helpful in teaching me to handle money. I learned to use the telephone making business calls for him. He was very kind. He taught me how to price can goods, utilizing the invoice to break down the cost of a case to a "per can price." I found out about the job because we shopped there. I made twenty-five dollars working nine-hour days, six days a week.

Grandma's first time seeing television was when she worked for Rosemary's Catering. It was a WOAI preview. WOAI-TV was San Antonio's first television station going on air in 1949. Grandma was twenty-six. Let that sink in . . . not watching television at all until the age of twenty-six! I realize there are still places around the world that don't have television and certain cultures that don't watch television at all, but that is not the culture in which I grew up.

Grandma only owned one television at a time. Streaming television programs on your smartphone wasn't an option.

Smartphones didn't exist! I remember her having two TVs her whole life, but she told me about another one—her first. John and Myrtle Sullivan gave it to her and Grandpa when my uncle Joe was small. Mr. Sullivan was a co-worker of Grandpa's when he worked for H. B. Zachry. The first television I remember was the large console they owned at their fancy house in University Hills. It lasted over twenty years. When it died, it was cheaper to buy a new one than to get it fixed.

Grandma never let what could have become excuses get in her way. She always did what was necessary. If it was in her skill set, she did it herself. If not, she delegated well. Either way, she knew how to get things done.

I was not a very good gardener. I preferred working with the cattle. Everyone laughed, for I said the cows had personalities; of course, each had a name. They seemed to answer to their names. Caring for them was a full-time job. Some were kind, good mothers to their calves. I remember a pleasant time when a young heifer, due to give birth to her first calf, was not with the herd and it was beginning to rain. I went to find her. She had just had her calf, and it couldn't stand. She was in a ravine that would fill with water when it rained, so I picked up her calf and carried it back to the pen. She followed close behind. Some of the cows gathered around when we arrived at the pen and helped the calf get up to nurse. Things turned out great. One cow, I remember well, was mean and would push her way to get to the feed. Once she knocked me into a gate, running a stob [a stake used for fencing] into my thigh at the hip. It seemed I was always getting hurt, for I was doing adult jobs.

My poor mother never knew what to expect. My first hit [injury] happened when I was only a year or so. It was too cold to take me along during milking, so my brother was left to watch me. He claimed I began to cry, so he started to jump on the bed to quiet me. I hit my head on the iron bedpost. I had to take stitches.

The year before Dad died, he took us to his hometown of Hallettsville, Texas, to stay with his cousin. I was in terrible pain and didn't consider it much of a vacation. We seldom talked about or planned vacations, for we had to attend to all the chores. Remember, we milked the cows and fed the animals every day. I don't remember much about this trip because it was right after I burned my arms with hot grease. Mama had left bacon cooking on the wood stove. I tried to move the skillet to keep it from catching fire. Mama coated my arms with salve and wrapped them in gauze. I started running fever, and Dad decided he was going to get Epsom salt to help bring it down. They consulted Dr. McCullough, who had a dairy just north of our farm.

Once, I had a bone infection from a cow's kick. Another time, while cutting cane for the calves, I cut my ankle with a sickle, almost severing the primary leader[artery] to my foot. When I was eight years old, I had my appendix removed.

One summer, my uncle Walter Appelt and his three kids, Dorothy, Betty, and Clifford, spent time with us. My cousin Clifford and I were the same age. We were trying to ride shotgun [in the front passenger seat] for my brother, Lawrence [who was driving]. Clifford pushed me while trying to get in the truck, and I slipped, hitting the running board. I fractured my tailbone and suffered for years, as it was slow to heal. The country doctor had an office mostly in his home where we went. If needed, he came to the house of a sick person. Operations were performed at Santa Rosa Hospital. I soon learned to forget the ills, for many blessings came my way and the show of God's love. For God had the solution before I had the problem.

Wow! Let's talk about her faith of knowing that God had the solution to her problems before they even came her way. This is true for us too! God sees the shadows in our lives, but He can also see what is hiding in them. God can see in the dark. He is light. Grandma's faith allowed her to move on to the next right thing, never dwelling too long where she didn't want to take root.

"You can make an excuse, or you can make a difference, but you can't make both."[18] At first glance, that looks like a great tweet—something to encourage you to stop making excuses and start making a difference. The reality is, excuses or not, you're making a difference. You're making an impact on those around you with your excuses or without. It comes down to what kind of impact you want to make. Our potential to make a positive impact in the lives of others is directly related to our willingness to focus. Our job isn't to make excuses for what we can't do, but instead to focus on what we can do and do it well! Stay in your lane! As Jim Collins says, "Find the right seat on the right bus."[19]

Think about the kind of legacy you want to leave behind. Do you want to be remembered as the person that always had an excuse? Excuses are a way to shed responsibility—a way to cast blame on something or someone other than yourself. Maturity isn't about age, it's about responsibility. When you take responsibility, you push through the barriers. You do what you can, and you delegate the rest. We're not all gifted the same way. There are things that I have no interest in learning to do and activities I physically can't do. Grandma confided that she had hopes of becoming a nurse when she grew up. However, her circumstances led her to become a cook.

*My mother's oldest brother, a railroad engineer, and
his wife offered to send me to nursing school in Sweetwater,
Texas, where they lived. Mother said no, for she was afraid
I would become a housekeeper, for they only had a son,
and he was away in college. Also, my mother lived by all
Catholic laws and rules, and my uncle's wife was Jewish.
I believe that influenced my mom.*

Grandma realized she could care for people through cooking, just as she'd done from a young age. Based on the gifts she'd
been given, she chose to weave her world. We must look at our
circumstances as not happening to us, but for us. *Circumstance*
is not a dirty word. Conditions can change. Just as Grandma
went from hand-me-down dresses to owning her own business,
what matters is how we use what we've been given. God uses
our circumstances to grow us into who He created us to be.
We need to be good stewards of our experiences.

Craig Groeschel shares about excuses in his leadership
podcast. He says, as leaders, we have to stop discounting or
qualifying our people, and we need to stop using the forbidden
phrase, "Our people won't or don't," or "Our team never."[20]
In doing this, we're casting blame on our people. Instead,
he teaches that we need to take responsibility as leaders and
lead them well. I agree! We also need to lead ourselves well.
Whether you consider yourself a leader or not, you're the only
person responsible for the way you conduct yourself. We need
to stop the excuses and start taking responsibility.

Be a good steward of the gifts you've been given. Not
of the ones you wish you had or the gifts you covet in your
neighbor, but the gifts *you've* been given. Not the gifts others
think you have, but your authentic gifts. Being a good steward
of your gifts means to leverage them for maximum impact
and influence.

One of my jobs, while I creatively avoided writing, was in sales. Darren thought, because I'm outgoing, talkative, and persuasive, that I would be an excellent fit for a sales position that was available. I interviewed and accepted the job, but soon realized that I didn't like what I was selling. I do have those traits Darren saw in me, but I knew I wasn't supposed to be using them to sell advertising. Ultimately, I was letting my excuses win. I wasn't good enough or sufficiently educated to be a writer. I wasn't a "somebody." Those excuses, among many, led me to creatively avoid my heart's deepest desire. Scripture tells us to "Take delight in the Lord, and He will give you the desires of your heart."[21] It doesn't say anything about being good enough or educated enough.

It brings me back to Grandma: "God knows the solution before I have the problem." *That* is delighting in Him! She knew He would take care of everything. She did her part by serving others with what He gave her, and He blessed her efforts with success in every area of her life.

Just like Grandma, I want to help others. My method looks differently than hers. My skills are different. Anyone that knows me, knows I can't cook. Grandma knew how to cook because she'd been doing it for her family since her father died, when she was just nine. She took the best skill she had and poured herself into helping others through that gift. No excuses. She worked her way up from the grocery store, learning about pricing, to working at the Pig Stand, a small restaurant. Then she went on to work for Rosemary's Catering and Tommy's Catering, until she opened her successful restaurant and catering business, Katherine's. She catered for many companies in San Antonio, including the Lone Star Brewery. In 1973, the San Antonio Restaurant Association acknowledged her success with a "Tastes of the Town" award.

Katherine's Restaurant   *Grandma in the kitchen
at her restaurant*

Lawrence; Grandpa's mother, Ruth; Grandpa; and Grandma

Katherine's Restaurant

* CATERING   *** PRIVATE PARTY ROOMS**

For more Information   Ask our Cashier

HOUSE SPECIALTIES

Chicken Fried Steak	$1.69	Breaded Veal Cutlet	$1.69
with Cream Gravy		with Brown Gravy	

Southern Fried Chicken ———————— $1.69
(3 pieces)

Above served with Tossed Green Salad (Choice of dressing)
French Fries or Baked Potato Hot Rolls & Butter

MEXICAN DISHES

Mexican Dinner ———————— $1.60
2 Enchiladas - 1 Beef Taco -
Beans - Rice

Tamales ———————— $1.60
with Meat Chili
Tortillas - Hot Sauce

Enchiladas (3) ———————— $1.25
with Chili & Cheese

Deluxe Mexican Dinner ———————— $2.00
2 Enchiladas - 1 Beef Taco
1 Tamale - Beans - Rice - Chili
Tortillas - Chalupa - Hot Sauce

Crisp Beef Tacos (3) ———————— $1.00

Chili Bowl ———————— $ .79

BAR-B-QUE

Sliced Beef Brisket ———————— $1.80

Sausage Plate ———————— $1.60

Mixed Bar-B-Que ———————— $2.00
Brisket & Sausage

All above served with Ranch Style Beans -
Potato Salad - Onion - Pickles - Rye Bread

Sliced Bar-B-Que on Bun ———————— $ .95
with Chips

All side orders of Vegetables
or Pinto Beans ———————— $ .35

SALADS

Chef Salad ———————— $1.65
Ham - Roast - Cheese -
Tomatoes - Eggs
(One's a meal)

Tossed Salad ———————— $ .50

Cottage Cheese & Fruit ———————— $ .60

Potato Salad ———————— $ .40

Choice of Dressing

All Items Available for Take-Out

Banquet and Business Meeting Facilities for all Hours

Varied Luncheon Menus Daily

Call 533-7511   Breakfast 6 AM

DESSERTS

Pie ———————— $ .35

Ice Cream ———————— $ .25

Pie a la Mode ———————— $ .50

Look at those prices!

I had no favorite foods. I just loved food and loved to cook. I remember when I went to work as a cashier at the Pig Stand in 1946. I became assistant manager, and one of my responsibilities was to check the waitresses' and carhops' orders. Some foods I didn't know about, like shrimp cocktail. I quickly learned about so many foods.

Instead of focusing on her lack of knowledge, Grandma focused on learning. She used what she already had to fulfill her dream of helping others. Excuses are lies we tell ourselves. I don't know about you, but I don't like liars. Tell me the truth, in love, before you tell me a lie. Unfortunately, we lie to ourselves by making promises we have no idea how to keep or by comparing ourselves to others. Comparison without action is just pity. Either we're creating our own pity party, or we pity others. If you focus on what God calls you to do, there is no need to compare yourself to anyone. Stop judging others. Playing God is not our calling. Stop concerning yourself with the opinions of others. You serve God first and others only through Him.

After Grandma retired from her restaurant and catering business, she was invited on exotic hunting trips to cook for the hunters. She went on to work for the Elks Lodge for a time. Her connections there allowed her to help and serve others, as well. At her funeral in 2017, a man arrived by bicycle to pay his respects. I will never forget this man. She made such an impact on his life that he rode his bike in the dark to her visitation. We didn't get much time to chat, but he shared that he worked with Grandma at the Elks Lodge.

This sweet man handed me a note as he left that read, "Please remember to let me know the date and time of the book launch party." He included his name, address, and phone number. (I made my son drive him home, since he had a truck to put the man's bike in.) I still sit in awe, thinking of the impact Grandma had on him and that he would go through such effort to reach out to us. I look forward to seeing him again. This man is an excellent example of knowing what you want and not letting excuses get in the way. He rode his bicycle in the dark through San Antonio—population 1.5 million![22] No excuses!

Another guest at the visitation was a woman on a mission. A very successful business woman Grandma had once worked for was in her nineties, but she was all dolled-up and there to pay her respects. So powerful to see one successful woman coming to pay respects to another woman of significant influence. No excuses.

The truth is, we're making our lives way too complicated. We have to trash the excuses, fears, and excess we're burying ourselves under trying to creatively avoid what we've been called to do. Live your truth. We have to stop comparing and start learning from one another. As Bob Goff says, "We won't be distracted by comparison if we are captivated with purpose."[23]

Doubts are like birds; they may fly over, but don't let them nest. Don't reason your way out of the will of God. Let God have His way in your life.

There is no such thing as perfect this side of heaven, so stop letting the pursuit of perfection hold you back. Everyone makes mistakes. Let your life be about people, passion, and purpose. The world is waiting for you to get past your excuses. Your circle is tired of hearing your excuses. Maybe you've been waiting for a sign or a push? Well, here it is. No more hesitation, no more procrastination. Just go for it. Create a beautiful legacy, not excuses.

I will not be held back by past mistakes,
but will rise with the lessons.
#WorthSaving

CHAPTER 5

Lies We Avoid

*"Don't be afraid that your life will end,
be afraid it will never begin"*

~ Anonymous

Growing up, my life motto was, "It's my life. If all those around me died tomorrow, it'd still be my life, and I'll have to live with the decisions I've made." Sounds kind of morbid, but that's what I would say to myself when making important decisions. I was trying to determine if I was deciding for *me* or for someone else. Before I was a Christian, I saw my life as my own, and I would often make decisions based on my motto. I can even recall sharing my motto with people making decisions in their own lives. I would tell them, "Look, this is your life, and if everyone around you dies tomorrow, you'll have to live with this decision. Can you live with it? Choose wisely."

While I still see some validity in my motto, I now understand that my life doesn't belong to me. I gave it to Christ years ago. I still feel you shouldn't make decisions based on the opinions of others, but I firmly believe you should look to God. If you're screening your choices through Him, and everyone around you died, you could trust you've made the right decision based on your purpose in Christ.

After moving away from my hometown of San Antonio—away from all I've ever known, all my friends and family—I questioned my decision. I thought to myself, if everyone around me died right now—Darren, his family, and my youngest daughter (the only one still at home)—what would I do? Did I make the right decision? It was probably the closest I've come to hearing God audibly speak to me. He spoke loudly to my heart and reminded me that He called me here.

Before relocating, Darren and I prayed, and prayed some more. The decision wasn't just if we should move, but where should we move, as well. We had another opportunity, which we strongly considered. It's a dream destination that we visit every summer—my little slice of heaven on earth. The decision was huge for our family and me. I was leaving behind so much, but I felt God telling me so clearly that it was time and this was the place. We prayed for God's will to be done in our lives, asking Him to show us clearly if He wanted us to move. He did, so we did. It was time for me to move into a different area of ministry, and I felt God calling me to East Texas.

The day I questioned the move, it was as if God wrapped His loving arms around me and whispered in my ear, "For I know the plans I have for you . . . remember? Do not fear for I called you to this place for a purpose." I've never felt so at peace. I guess it's time to rewrite my motto. It should read more like this: "My life belongs to Christ. If everyone around me dies tomorrow, are my decisions going to be pleasing to Him?" When you're fearful about your future, you are not including God in your future. You can either be a worrier, or include God and be a warrior!

We are not victims of our circumstances when we allow God to use them to grow us. As I was thinking about people in my life, some Christians and some not, my heart was breaking for them. Some of them have no self-worth, no self-esteem, and no sense of belonging. I can see a better life for them—better opportunities with less pain. I have a vision in my head of what their life could be like, just as parents do with their children. We want them to grow up to have a safe, healthy, and productive life. As they start to cross into different stages of their lives—from childhood to teens, from teens to adulthood—we as parents have a vision of what their lives could be. If you're a parent, you know it doesn't matter what we want because, as your children grow, they have their own desires and dreams. But sadly, they also have their fears. Sometimes people stop dreaming altogether. They become hopeless because they've tried and failed or have been discouraged. They are too fearful or busy to reach for their dreams, or they've lost sight of it all together.

As God usually does when I'm reflecting on the lives of others, He reminded me that I don't always follow my dreams. His vision for my life is so grand that I can't even comprehend it. I've been guilty of allowing my doubts and fears to make me a victim of my circumstances too. So how do we go from victim to victorious? We lean in.

You see, beyond anything we can hope for or dream, God has a purpose and vision for each of our lives. We need to tap into God's plans, not the story our parents have for us or the one the world creates. Before we were born, He knew what He wanted us to do. The problem is, we don't see ourselves through God's eyes. We usually see ourselves through the lives of those around us, through our failures, through the media, and through the world. We let the enemy cloud the vision God has given us. We need to find out how He feels about us and start seeing ourselves through His eyes.

In John 5, Jesus encounters a man who had been sick for over thirty-eight years. Jesus asks him, "Do you want to get well?"[24] The man immediately replies with excuses about how he couldn't get to the pool to receive healing and how others keep getting in before him. Jesus commands him, "Get up; pick up your mat and walk."[25] The man complies and is healed. When he let go of the excuses, he could accept the healing that had been waiting for him for years. The man allowed his stories to keep him from what Jesus had planned for him.

There is the pain of change and the pain of staying the same. If we let God work on the inside, it's going to reflect on the outside. It starts with believing God can work within us and through us. If we remain fearful and let our excuses overpower our actions, we're likely to miss the blessings waiting for us. We need to question fear when it presents itself. Don't accumulate it, don't make excuses for it.

Let's talk about what fear is for a moment. Fear should act as a pause button in your life. When you feel fearful, you should pause and ask why. Fear is not unhealthy, but how we deal with it can be. The fear of God is healthy. Some call it reverential. We should show the utmost respect for God; however, fear and respect are two different things.

It's not enough to know *about* Jesus; we have to seek to know Him fully. When we began to understand the power and character of God, we learn the difference between fear and respect. I respected God and all His marvelous creation even before I began a relationship with Jesus. Once I started to understand His character and that He is entirely God and wholly in control, I began to understand fear. He created us and the world we live in, and He can take us out of it at any time. Some people can't comprehend why I quit college the way I did, or why I'm so passionate about pursuing writing. My answer is simple—fear. I understand the power of God in my limited human ability to do so. I fear Him because I believe all of His Word, not just the fluffy parts that make me feel good. He corrects those that walk with Him just like a parent should correct a child. He wants the best for us, but to receive it we need to be obedient to the things He asks of us.

Let me give you an example of what I mean: we could google "promises of God" and get verse after verse of what God says He will do for us. The problem is, people don't read these verses in context. They usually remember the promise but little else. For example, here's a promise of God from Isaiah 40:29: "He gives power to the weak and strength to the powerless." Raise your hand if you need some power. Yep, my hand went up too, but let's finish reading.

Let's start in verse 26, where Isaiah reminds us who God is, and see if you can catch what I'm talking about. "Look up into the heavens. Who created all the stars? He brings them out like an army, one after another, calling each by its name. Because of His great power and incomparable strength, not a single one is missing. O Jacob, how can you say the Lord does not see your troubles? O Israel, how can you say God ignores your rights? Have you never heard? Have you never understood? The Lord is the everlasting God, the Creator of all the earth. He never grows weak or weary. No one can measure the depths of His understanding. He gives power to the weak and strength to the powerless. Even the youths will become weak and tired, and young men will fall in exhaustion. But those who trust in the Lord will find new strength. They will soar high on wings like eagles. They will run and not grow weary. They will walk and not faint."

Did you catch it? First Isaiah reminds us of who God is and of His power. Then he challenges us, asking if we've heard and understand? Next, he expounds on God's strength and tells us how we can tap into it. This is the most important part. Don't miss it! He says, "But those . . ." He's talking about *us*. "Those who trust in the Lord . . . " It's a relationship. We have to do our part. Have you ever been in a one-sided relationship? How did that turn out? It's never fun to be the only one engaged in communication or invested in a friendship. God wants us to be involved and invested in our relationship with Him.

While on the way home from a road trip, after hearing people take God's name in vain over and over for three days, I asked God why people do that. I was apologizing on their behalf and asking God to forgive them. I prayed the same prayer Jesus did on the cross: "Forgive them, Father, they know not what they do."[26] God made it so clear to me that the reason they used His name in vain was because they're not friends with Him. Think about that for a moment . . . Would you use your best friend's name as a cuss word? That's how close God wants to be with us. He doesn't want us to flippantly refer to Him when someone cuts us off in traffic or things don't go our way. He wants us to call on His name because we're in a relationship with Him.

When we seek to know Him, His character—to understand and trust in His plan for us—fear subsides. This is where reverence comes in. We know that God has the power to take us out in one heartbeat, but we also understand His love for us. He has great plans for us. He is waiting on us. By faith, we've already been rescued from hell, shame, and fear! God didn't save us from the pit so we could create a prison for ourselves. God's Word tells us over 365 times, "Do Not Fear." I think He is trying to make a point. He doesn't want us to be fearful, He wants us to be obedient. In that obedience, if we're fearful, should be a healthy pause to remind us of Who is in control and Who called us. "The fears of the wicked will be fulfilled; the hopes of the godly will be granted."[27]

In speaking to my teenager about her plans to move to a foreign country for a year, I assured her that her father and I would not get in God's way and would support her in every way. I reminded her that it's hard for us to let our teenager move to the middle of the rainforest. She replied, "Don't you think I'm terrified?" It was strangely comforting knowing she was scared. I knew that she was fully relying on God. It wasn't just some fun adventure she decided to go on. It was a call that she was answering out of obedience. It was a healthy fear. She knows her place and she knows His.

Don't wait to pursue your dreams until nothing is opposing you. There will always be a mountain to climb, or one only God can move. He may be using that mountain to equip you to accomplish your dreams. Stop wasting your time being afraid. Your most significant act of obedience will be to take action in the face of fear. "Remember, it is sin to know what you ought to do and then not do it."[28] Love others through your obedience until the fear disappears. My pastor says, "Courage is the judgment that something else is more important than one's fear."[29] We have to discern what that something else is. What is more important than our fear? What would make us trash creative avoidance, control, excess, excuses, and fear? There is something more important, more valuable—I'd even say *eternal*—at stake.

Stop trying to fix what only God can fix. Stop doing things that are utterly useless. Worrying is useless. It doesn't change the outcome, and it slows down the input. Worrying is using your imagination to create what you don't want. Imagination is where answers come to find a way out. If you're asking yourself what your future holds, use your imagination wisely.

Your choices should be a reflection of your hopes, not your fears. Whatever your excuse is, it's a seducer waiting to lure you to complacency. "You will be accepted if you do what is right. But if you refuse to do what is right, then watch out! Sin is crouching at the door, eager to control you. But you must subdue it and be its master."[30] Don't let the enemy use fear to steal your power. You're either pitiful or powerful; you can't be both. You decide. If you could only see yourself the way God sees you. He understands what He created—a powerful being made in His image.

If you want to avoid criticism or self-limiting beliefs, then don't do anything with your life. Otherwise, get up, be bold, stand out, and know God has your back. Use your last fear as a chance to grow your faith. You've paused long enough. It's time to move. "Success is when the passion inside your heart is bigger than the fear inside your head."[31]

The long-running television show *The Biggest Loser*[32] always inspired me. I enjoy watching people overcome whatever is holding them back. The basic premise (if you haven't seen it) is that a group of contestants compete to see who can lose the most weight over the season. During the episode before the finale, the personal trainer takes the contestant up to the scale and shows them a cardboard cutout of themselves before they began the weight-loss program. One particular season, the winner was a female named Ali. As Ali was standing next to her life-size cut-out a whole ninety-nine pounds lighter than before, her trainer asked her what was different between then and now. With a smile on her face, Ali professed three simple words: "I love myself." When she spoke, it was as if the Holy Spirit finished the sentence for me: "Enough for everyone." *I love myself enough for everyone.*

One of my biggest fears has been that I'm not enough. I'm not educated enough, smart enough, spiritual enough, et cetera. My desire to be loved and accepted fueled my desire to be enough. The moment Ali spoke those three words changed me. It was blatantly apparent that I needed to love myself enough. I needed to love myself enough for everyone—for those who've hurt me or offended me, for those I felt should love me but didn't show me love, and to fill in the gaps for those trying to love me in their own way. It's often the people who we feel are supposed to love us the most who can cause the most pain or disappointment.

By loving ourselves enough for everyone, we're no longer seeking the approval or acceptance of those around us. We stop seeking the approval of false gods. Only then can we freely focus on those we're called to serve, whether they love us or not. We can't control how someone else feels about us. We shouldn't be codependent, changing our behavior to receive the acceptance of others. We should focus on our gifts and the One who gave them to us. Like the song "How You Live" says, "Make peace with God and make peace with yourself. 'Cause, in the end, there's nobody else."[33]

Don't confine God to what He's already done. He is not finished with you yet. I'm so thankful for this fact! He won't be finished with us until we're face to face with Him. Don't let that discourage you. He has already provided all that we need to accomplish His plan for us. He knows our needs before we ever cry out to Him. He is molding us, awakening us to who He created us to be. It's time we move out of the comfort zone and into the courage zone. He goes before us. There is no need to fear. Turn your fear into fortitude. If we want a new thing, we have to let go of the old habits, mindsets, dreams, and stories.

We need to move from our comfort zone—or what should be called the fear zone—to the God zone. I refer to this "zone" as His peace. We find courage in His peace. When His peace fills me, the words flow, as I write almost without thought.

There's a scene in the movie *For the Love of the Game*[34] when the character played by Kevin Costner is on the pitcher's mound. The crowd is cheering, some even taunting. Suddenly, for him, it's quiet. He flashes back to a time when he was playing ball with his father. Peace seems to come over him. His next pitch is perfect. The crowd is still noisy, but he tunes them out. He is in the zone—a place where it's just him and his gift. No fear, just his dad reminding him that he can do it.

Our Heavenly Dad is always right there in the zone, waiting to tell you that you can do it. The more time we spend in the God zone hearing from Him, the easier it is to find our way back there. The more familiar we get with leaning in and trusting God, the easier it becomes. Our courage multiplies as we see God at work. Turn your focus from your fears to your faith. If you believe God is who He says He is, then start acting like it.

Stop seeking the approval of false gods.
#WorthSaving

PART 2

Treasure

CHAPTER 6

Begin with Inspiration

"Dear outsiders, even the most beautiful of wildflowers are considered weeds in the wrong gardens—what another thinks of you does not dictate your value."

~ Beau Taplin

I don't know about you, but I love a fascinating biography. I love learning where people came from and what they're doing with what God gave them. My favorites are stories in which people triumph over obstacles. Overcoming is a choice. It's a state of mind and being. Your perspective is what changes, not your circumstances. Scripture tells us we're more than conquerors. No matter if you believe that or not, you have a choice to make. You can let your humble beginnings limit you or launch you.

Sadly, most of the time in our society, we're comparing our beginning to someone else's end. We judge ourselves by other people's highlight reel played out on social media. Seeing a successful person, but not learning how they made it, is like seeing an oak tree and forgetting it was once an acorn.

We need to quit holding back and nurture the seed God planted within us. Seeds are for beginnings, and seeds are for multiplying. If the first seed never blooms, it will never reproduce. If it never blooms, it will die within us. We are responsible for the seed God planted in our hearts. What will you do with all that you've been given—the good, the bad, and the ugly?

We must not be jealous of what others have, especially if we're not willing to do what they did to get it. The sacrifices, sweat, and tears that go into reaching your full potential are often only seen by those closest to us. Many times, even they don't know what is going on under the surface.

One time, a woman from a small group I lead told me when she feels like she is under attack from the enemy, she sends him to my house. I was appalled! Of course, I asked her why she would do such a thing. She said she thought I could handle it better than she could. Boy, if she only knew! My struggle is a daily one. If we could pull back the curtains of our hearts, our hearts would break for one another. The truth is we're all going through something. The difference is where you are in the process. The enemy is unrelenting in his effort to render us insignificant. We must realize the enemy only goes after what is valuable. When I say my struggle is a daily one, that is not an exaggeration!

Preparing to talk on stage recently in front of about two hundred people, I asked my husband for prayer and told him I was nervous. He said that I better get over it if I want to speak on bigger stages and more often. It stopped me in my tracks. NONE of what I am doing is within my own strength. I am scared beyond scared about speaking and sharing my stories with the world. But God . . . He called me to this, and He walks me through it. It is not by my strength but by His!

I thought I was pretty transparent about my struggles, fears, and failures, but people only see what's in front of them. They see me going up to speak when they are afraid of public speaking; they see me teaching when they don't feel called to teach; they see me publishing a book, or whatever it is they deem successful for me, and think that I have it all together or that things come easy for me. Wrong! Don't be fooled by the success you see in others. We all fall short. We all face fears. We all start somewhere and with a past, some more horrific than others.

When we're transparent, we connect our hearts to others. People trust the vulnerable places in our souls. If we put our weakness in the light, then we control it rather than letting someone else call it out. Don't waste time comparing yourself to who you thought you were supposed to be. Embrace who you are. You already have all that you need.

We must learn to treasure our beginnings, as well as the start of something new. It's an adventure that will become a great story, no matter the outcome. We may not be able to control the journey, but we can control our attitude. Beginnings can be scary. Not knowing what to do, what direction to go, where the resources will come from, or what the outcome will be, often leads us to perfection paralysis.

We're known by our fruit, not by how well-manicured the tree is. Fruit doesn't come without seeds. The fruit doesn't have to be perfect to produce seeds. It just has to do what it was meant to do: grow. We all need a little pruning along the way. No one starts as a mighty oak.

Grandma's beginnings were something out of a history book. Sometimes, during our morning chats, I would stare in awe of her. Knowing all that she lived through, all that transpired in the world during her ninety-three years, blows my mind. She shared a bit about her humble beginnings with me. These were also the first words written on that tattered notebook she handed me when she asked me to write about all the good in her life.

My Memories of a Journey Through a Very Full Life, Observations, and Views of People and an Ever-changing World

Life began in a loving home with parents of great hopes and strength, of hard work, of faith in God and loyalty to country. Dad worked at an insane asylum on South Presa and Mom at Santa Rosa Hospital in the sewing room. Daddy was offered a job cooking at the Railroad Hospital in Houston and asked Mama to go with him. Mr. Lawrence was the head of the Railroad Hospital and took care of Mama while Daddy went back to stay with his parents because he had typhoid fever. When they were to raise a family, they decided to go to the country and became dairy farmers.

*JULIUS JOSEPH APPELT AND MARY KATHERINE RIPPS
WEDDING PICTUTE*

The farm was sixteen acres on Chavaneaux [pronounced SHA-VIN-AWE] and Highway 281 in south San Antonio. Sixteen heifers started the dairy. Lawrence was born in the barn. He was named after Mr. Lawrence. I was born in the house. I was named after my grandmother and Mother's middle name. My middle name, Florence, was just a name my mom liked. All four of her children had either a first or middle name starting with an "F."

When my father opened a country store on the side of the house, no electricity was in the surrounding area, so my dad built a small generator for lights and refrigeration. I remember weighing and packing beans, rice, and sugars and helping in the store at five or six years old. Other daily chores included feeding the calves and chickens, gathering eggs, washing dishes and clothes, ironing, sweeping, and changing the beds. As I grew, any and all chores became my responsibility. Bringing the cows from the pasture, we used a whip to keep them in line, but mostly just walked with them. I helped with whatever was needed, often bringing in wood for the stoves.

We had very few covers for the windows. There were screens on the windows and doors. We opened them to cool the house. We cooked with the wood stove and had two large wood-burning heaters. I didn't have running water until I moved to town at twenty-one years of age.

The Depression began, and my father was very ill. He died in 1933. I was nine years old. My mother was left alone with four small children: Lawrence was sixteen, I was nine, Josephine was five, and Ferdinand (who we called "Ferdie") was fourteen months. Shortly before my dad died, the road to our property was to become a major highway to South Texas, Corpus Christi, and Laredo, so our home had to be moved. The Highway Department bought the front of our property and left us the dairy. After they split our property, we herded cattle over Highway 281 to be milked daily.

Grandma's mom, Josephine, Grandma, Lawrence, and Ferdie

Early on, I realized there were many single parents, mostly because death took one at an early age. Families were helped by grandparents, uncles, and aunts, much like today. My favorite uncle, my mother's youngest brother, August Ripps, was close to her and helped after my father died. Her brother Willy also did a lot for her. My mother's sister Margaret cared for her parents (my grandparents). When she was thirty-nine, both her parents passed away. She married Albert Richardson, a G.I. (slang for an American soldier starting around World War II; they considered themselves "Government Issue"). They moved to New York and had a son, Donald Richardson.

I remember my mother quit speaking German in public, not wanting to be known as German during the war. No relatives ever lived with us, but Mother befriended the Bollinger family. After Mrs. Bollinger died, her youngest son, Densley, lived with us for some time. He went to work at Kelly Field during WWII and got Lawrence a job there, as well.

Everyone was very active at the many missions around San Antonio: restoring them, preserving them, and raising funds for such. I went to San Francisco de la Espada Mission when it opened as a school. My grandparents were influential in getting it opened by the bishop with the help of the Sisters of the Incarnate Word and Blessed Sacrament. I had an aunt who was a nun. I recall many happy times there, for many of my cousins attended, along with about a hundred children of Spanish farmers.

Mission Espada students in the 1930s

There, I learned to speak Spanish and taught the Spanish kids English. The only time I remember getting teased was when the Spanish kids would laugh at how I would say some of the words, but I finally learned to speak Spanish and was accepted by them. The nuns wanted all to speak English and would punish us for speaking Spanish on the playground; I was no exception. The only other punishment I ever remember was an occasional slap from my mother. Very few punishments happened in our family—everyone was too busy with chores.

81

School began at 8 A.M. Some days we attended Mass first. We had one hour for lunch and were out at 3 P.M. We would eat sack lunches, and I would sometimes trade for tortillas from friends. We only used books at school. They were never brought home. There was no such thing as "homework" given, as we had too many chores. We used an Indian Chief Tablet to take notes and write out lessons for the teacher to grade. We used a regular pencil with an eraser. The school had a sharpener in each room. We did not use pens, for there were only quills with ink, and those were for much higher grades. We wore anything we had. Everyone was too poor for school uniforms. I played the fife (similar to a piccolo) in the school's Drum and Fife Corps. We marched in the Battle of Flowers Parade. We did have corps uniforms.

Josephine, Grandma, and Lawrence

Grandma is the female not looking at the camera

front row: Josephine seated far right;
second row: Lawrence standing behind Josephine,
and Grandma sixth from right

*Lawrence far left; Grandma behind him
with her fife to her lips*

The young children were in a new part of the mission, built on to the main building that remained. The older grades were in a room next to a dome-shaped room that was a lookout. It had a hole in the rear wall for shooting. No floor, just dirt. The walls were mortar.

Some of the children received minimal schooling because they were needed to help with chores. Many went on to better their lives with hard work, observing, reading, and studying on their own. One of my teachers, Sister Simplica, saw I was able to handle more lessons than she was teaching the class. She gave me more, which helped, for I was not able to continue schooling.

I was needed to help at home after my father died. My mother was working daily, taking care of the dairy farm and home full-time, as well as raising us four kids. While in school, I made many friends. My closest friends were daughters of a Mexican family on the adjoining *farm. I was a bridesmaid at their weddings. I thought it an honor, for we were very close. Their father taught us a lot about growing vegetables. He was a very successful garden farmer.*

Grandma center, next to the bride. As tradition would have it, all bridesmaids wore white in order to confuse any evil spirits, safely disguising the bride among the group

Each year, on the feast of St. Francis in October, a week-long carnival fiesta was held. The men built the booths and tables. The women all gathered to cook a Mexican dinner with my mother to raise funds for the school. Mother was good at cooking tamales, beans, enchiladas, and Spanish rice. The ladies from church made the flour tortillas.

When I was in sixth grade, the nuns had six to eight girls dress in crepe skirts and perform a choreographed dance. The colors of the skirts were beautiful.

Holy Week was very busy, as well. Easter tradition included building and decorating the altar. Friday, we honored the stations of the cross. Saturday was set aside for blessing the holy water, and Sunday was a beautiful Mass. There were no plastic Easter egg hunts. When I was a child, plastic wasn't as available to the public as it is now. I didn't even know it had been invented.

Our Christmas tradition as a family was to attend Midnight Mass. We would cut down a cedar tree as our Christmas tree and hang up silk stockings. Gifts were always something we needed. In my home, as a child, both Christmas and Easter were a sacred time. All of our holidays included Mass. Thanksgiving was a great family meal day. We prepared for a couple of days before—pies, turkey, and all the trimmings. Halloween was just the eve of All Saints Day. Some boys played pranks like overturning outhouses. Holidays were always a great day because we had plenty of good food and family together. We would play bridge and poker card games, and play games with the children. On birthdays, Mama always made a cake decorated with candles.

When I was born, my dad had a large flatbed truck. He bought a Buick sedan in 1928. Some kids arrived by horse and buggies to school. I walked two miles each way every day. Then, my dad bought my brother and me a horse and buggy. Our buggy was a gig. It was a two-wheeled buggy with one seat that was pulled by one horse. At school, the boys would tie up the horses in a treed area, and, at lunchtime, they would walk them down [to the San Antonio River] for water. After Dad died, Mother bought a Chevy pickup. My grandfather would drive us to church in his Model T Ford.

Grandma on horseback—notice she's in a dress

My aunt Bobo, as we call her, introduced me to a unique place in Blanco, Texas. Buggies and carriages from around the world fill the Buggy Barn Museum. They have several gigs. It was such a thrill to see them in person. I could picture Grandma in her yellow feed-sack dress on her way to school. If you want to step back in time and see some beautiful bits of history, I recommend a trip. On display are rare wagons and buggies dating from the 1860s to early 1900s. Major motion pictures, including *True Grit, Lonesome Dove,* and *There Will Be Blood,* used some of their buggies, carriages, and wagons.[35]

During one of my trips home to San Antonio, Jenifer and I took Grandma to visit the old farm property, which is now home to a major hotel chain. We also toured San Francisco de la Espada School, known to the locals as "Mission Espada." I will never forget wheeling Grandma into the "classroom" area that adjoined the old fort lookout. A large photograph hung on the wall of students sitting at desks, all facing the front, with a nun watching over them. As I read the information next to the picture, I realized Grandma's younger sister, Josephine, was one of those students! I asked Grandma if any of the children looked familiar, and she pointed to Josephine. I wished that picture was of Grandma, but I felt honored that my great-aunt was connected to history in such a fantastic way. I couldn't believe my eyes. In my mind, Mission Espada ranks right up there with the Alamo!

Grandma and me at Mission Espada. Josephine is the second girl in the middle row in the picture hanging on the wall

Mission San Francisco de la Espada was moved to the San Antonio River Valley from East Texas in 1731, along with two other San Antonio missions—Mission San Juan and Mission Concepción. Founded initially as Mission San Francisco de los Tejas near Augusta, Texas, it was established to convert the local indigenous tribes to Christianity and to protect the

Spanish frontier from French incursions. Mission Espada represents the most complete mission complex of all of the San Antonio missions.

Mission Espada, along with the four other San Antonio missions, comprises the largest concentration of Spanish colonial missions in North America, and they have been named a World Heritage Site.[36] This is a rare honor that has only been bestowed upon twenty-three sites in the United States at the time of this writing. These missions are the first World Heritage Site in Texas. (Other notable sites include Machu Picchu in the Andes Mountains of Peru; Stonehenge in Wiltshire, England; and the Taj Mahal in India.) Four of the missions (not including the Alamo) are active parishes, holding Catholic Mass every Sunday.

As we toured the Mission Espada grounds, Grandma told us that the students would go into the church during the school day for chapel, and this was where her family attended Mass on Sundays. She also pointed out the "creek," also known as the San Antonio River, where the boys watered the horses at lunchtime. The way the fort is built provides a courtyard-type area between the school section of the building and the church, with the river in the distance. Grandma explained that this is where they would play during recess.

It's amazing all that Grandma went on to accomplish in her life with limited schooling. Her education was hands-on hard work. It started at the farm. Being the eldest girl, she was responsible for many of the household chores, in addition to farm chores. She mastered in taking what God gave her and making the most out of it. From her gifts and talents, to the simplest butter tub—everything had a purpose.

Grandma became the family cook out of necessity when her dad died, and she had no choice but to help with her siblings. Her parents, Julius Joseph and Mary Katherine Ripps Appelt, both native Texans, were cooks in previous careers, so she saw that it was a viable job. That which was born out of necessity became her way of loving people. She served others through cooking. She was gifted, and her abilities became her gift to others. Let your gifts become a gift to others.

School sure has changed since Grandma attended. Even over the years between my being in school and my children attending school, much had changed. When I finished high school, attending college was expected of graduates, but not everyone did. I joined the United States Air Force instead of starting college right away. Currently, most high schoolers are getting dual credits for both college and high school classes before they even graduate. My youngest graduated high school a year early with fifteen college hours, while working and dancing on the school's dance team. For the most part, however, work experience isn't as prevalent in younger generations because the focus is on school and sports. A strong work ethic is essential in our family, and all of our children had jobs while attending high school and college.

Before I graduated high school, I worked at least five different jobs and even managed a small retail shop. I'm part of a rare group who enjoys school and work. I enjoy learning. I've also realized that I use learning as creative avoidance. For example, sometimes I find joy in reading a book about writing rather than writing. Remember that college story in chapter one? An excuse people often use is that they need more knowledge or information before they start something. Learning is growing, and that is always a good thing. We're either growing or dying. We must, however, be careful not to use learning as an excuse.

This book was written all over the place. From airports to coffee shops, libraries, hotels, family members' houses, and, of course, my studio. In the beginning, I was meeting with a writing friend of mine on a weekly basis. We would meet in coffee shops or restaurants to catch up on life and hold each other accountable for our writing. Then we would attempt to shut up long enough to write. One particular night, on the patio of Panera Bread, she told me to be careful not to stifle the Spirit by over-educating myself but, instead, to follow my calling. I agree with her and love that she saw a gift in me. She saw that God was trying to do something through me, and I was getting in the way of that.

When I was first asked to write this book, I prayed about it. How could I bring glory to God while honoring Grandma's precious life? While praying, this catchy title, *Save the Butter Tubs,* came to mind. The metaphor hadn't even entered my mind, just the words "save the butter tubs." Then I came across a teaching about how to title your books to get attention. I started second-guessing the title. I was letting human knowledge come before obedience. Now you know how that ended up!

Education is essential, but it's how we apply that knowledge that counts. We don't need to be overeducated and under obedient. "Most of us are educated way beyond the level of our obedience."[37] Success is doing the next right thing. Stop seeking what you've already been given.

I had the opportunity to hear a missionary at Youth with a Mission, Twin Oaks campus, who goes by the name "Maria from Korea," speak about success. She shared three main points:

Success < Holiness
Success < Submission
Success < Serving

Inspired by her message, I took notes as fast as I could with my smartphone. But I changed her points up a bit:

Holiness = Success
Submission = Success
Serving = Success

When you serve, you can't fail. God sees our hearts. Serving is an attitude of the heart. God calls us to know Him before we're to make Him known. Once walking with Him, we can submit and say, "Wherever you turn God, I'm there. Whatever you desire, I desire." God wants us to experience who He is through the process. He has indeed shown me who He is through the process of this book. Plans work, or they don't, but we can always choose to hear God, submit to God, and look for opportunities to serve. Even if we can't function to the degree we want to, we can still help. God can use us. Our obstacles can become opportunities.

Are you paying attention to God's heart? God knows what He's doing—we forget that way too often. Don't be so focused on what you think you want, that you miss the opportunities to serve that God has placed right in front of you. God invites you to follow Him and know His heart.

Most of the time, we're comparing someone else's excellent finish to our meager start or muddled middle. Stop comparing and focus on what you need to do. When you're comparing, you're showing up in other people's lives and not your own. Wishing you were someone else kind of defeats God's purpose of creating you. It's an insult to your Creator. Be you, bravely you.

You can let your humble beginnings limit you
or launch you.
#WorthSaving

CHAPTER 7

Belong in Your World

"To a great mind, nothing is little."

~ Sherlock Holmes

There are treasures all around us in simple things, simple ideas . . . and simply in people. When I imagine you, my reader, I wonder if you're like me, wondering about where you belong in this world and what belongings matter in your world. After Jenifer and I, along with other family members, went through every item in Grandma's house—every fork, piece of paper, picture, *everything*—I've thought more about physical belongings than ever before.

In my early twenties, my father's mother was diagnosed with cancer and given a short time to live. She had eight children, numerous grandchildren, and great-grandchildren. With help, she went through her belongings, mostly gifts and cards she'd received through the years. She designated a box for each of her children, returning what they had given her. If it was something Jenifer and I gave her, it went in my dad's box. It was sweet to reminisce. There were cards and gifts we had given her when we were small children. It was a touching gesture that I'll never forget.

I've started keeping separate keepsake boxes for my children and family that still send cards. Even if you don't get the items back to the giver, your loved ones might find it interesting to know the details of your precious belongings. My dad's mother physically wrote the gift-giver's name on the bottom of trinkets or on the backs of items. That's how she sorted them. I wish we would have done more of this with Grandma. We came across some interesting things when we packed up her estate. One item, in particular, was from Rock City, a place Darren and I visited in Tennessee. I hadn't realized anyone in my family had been to Tennessee, much less the same tourist attraction. I'd love to know the story behind it.

I don't know what it is about postcards, but I've always been in love with the idea of sending and receiving them. Maybe it's that they're an inexpensive way to share a piece of where you've been with the people you love. Perhaps it's the beautiful pictures that *make it big* and become postcards, or maybe it's something more. Listening to my favorite radio station in the car, they asked the "Survey of the Day" question: "They were once bestsellers, but experts say will soon be gone entirely. What are they?" Callers were responding with answers like CDs and iPods. The callers never guessed the correct answer. When the radio host announced that the answer was postcards, I sat clutching the steering wheel, looking straight ahead—stunned for a moment. I felt sad. I continued driving, puzzled by my reaction. I felt like someone was taking away a piece of me.

Okay, before you think my reaction was overly dramatic, let me explain. I'd just come back from vacation two weeks earlier, when I'd sent at least a dozen postcards to loved ones. I was a bit late getting the postcards in the mail this vacation because it was a holiday weekend. When I called Mom from the road, she asked me if I had sent any. Surprised, I told her about the holiday, and she said that Grandma was worried about how our trip was going because she hadn't received a postcard.

In researching for this book, I came across an old postcard tucked in with some family pictures. Sitting on Grandma's couch, I read it aloud and then passed it to her. The postcard brought back memories for Grandma and unlocked another piece of history for me. Not only did I have a picture of where this person had been (in this case, my grandfather), but I had his handwriting describing that moment in time. The postmark provided the date. The address and inscription unraveled a whole new story I'd never heard.

My grandparents lived apart early in their marriage while Grandpa worked in another city. I love how he addressed her: "My Dearest." He mentioned a check he had sent. He told her he was fine and hoped his baby was too. It turns out, she was pregnant with my uncle Joe at the time. He asked if she'd heard anything about an apartment she was looking into and told her when he'd be home. Just reading his words, I felt a connection with both of my grandparents that I had not felt before. That may have been the first time since my grandpa's passing that I had read his handwriting. A single four-by-six-inch piece of card stock from 1947 told a big story.

Technology is changing so quickly. Most people post vacation pictures to networking sites, where friends and family can see them instantly. I do too, but I also send that little piece of history back home via postcard. Postcards are an art form. They record history and can be quickly passed down from generation to generation. Social networking has its plus side—you don't have to worry about beating the postcards home from vacation because your posts are instant. It's not an either/or situation. We can do both!

A handwritten note is much more personal than a text or post online. It's your handwriting, your personality. It's a small gift, a treasure from where you've been. Social networking has become so familiar that sending and receiving postcards is now more special than ever. It takes more time and thought to pick out a particular card, write a sentiment, address it, stamp it, and mail it than it does to post a blanket vacation text and picture online. Which one says, "You're special" and "I'm thinking of you while I'm away?" Even if it's just for your child or your grandchildren to better understand you and your interests—it's worth the price of a stamp.

Commemorating an event or situation can be as simple as sending a postcard, or perhaps it's gifting someone with an empty Altoids tin. Once, while riding from lunch with my co-workers, one of them offered me an Altoids breath mint (the kind that comes in the tin with the little strip of wax paper in the bottom that folds neatly over the top). As I was reaching into the back seat to get a tiny mint, I accidentally grabbed the paper, flipping the entire tin of mints all over the car! I can still see the little white mints falling like raindrops in slow motion.

We all cried, we laughed so hard! The driver, the only man in the car, had to point out that when women laugh this hard, they tend to fan themselves with one hand while covering their mouth with the other. We four women looked around. It was true! We were all crying, laughing, and fanning ourselves with one hand and covering our mouths with the other. The truth in that moment only made us laugh harder!

When we arrived back at the office, we were still giggling and drying our eyes while waiting for the elevator. Another co-worker walked up. He hadn't been in the car and had no idea what we were laughing about. During the elevator ride, the tears flowed again as we retold the story to the outsider. He smiled at our laughter. We all agreed it was one of those "had-to-be-there" moments.

When I resigned from that position, my assistant gave me a sweet going-away gift. Tucked inside the gift bag, along with a beautiful journal, was an empty Altoids tin. We laughed and cried all over again. I still have that little tin. I keep it to remind myself that laughter is good for the soul. Sharing quirky moments with friends is fun.

The best part about that story is that it wasn't at the expense of anyone but me. It wasn't an inappropriate joke. It was just life. We should lighten up and enjoy those little moments more often. The best way I've found to do that is to cast our cares upon the Lord and enjoy the fellowship of others. I always look forward to spending time with the friends and family that keep me laughing. In a world of texting LOL (laughing out loud), how often do we honestly find ourselves laughing these days? Take time to enjoy moments with friends and commemorate them.

Learning as I go, I want to help other families capture those moments that may not seem important now, but someday they'll be thankful for taking the extra step. Take a lot of pictures. Post them on social media and send copies to close friends and family. In case of a catastrophic event, you'll be glad you can still access them. Begin thinking about how you can share your treasures with future generations. Don't let the stories die with you.

Jenifer shared some thoughts on documenting family history. Take pictures of your loved ones and their homes. Capture the way it looks inside and out while they are still living in it. If you're anything like me, you will need the photographs to help the memories come back. Jenifer even took pictures of a loved one's calendar while it was still hanging on the wall. She flipped through, taking photos of each month. Not only did this allow her to see what the person had marked down as important events, but she captured the birthdays of loved ones she hadn't known before.

Family history wasn't interesting to me when I was younger. I enjoyed spending time with family but didn't take the time to listen to the stories. Stories create memories. I recall Jenifer asking me about St. Joseph's Parish in San Antonio, Texas. She asked if I knew where it was and if I'd been inside. I answered, "Of course!" I walked right by it every day for years when I worked in downtown San Antonio. I peeked in a time or two to see what such an elaborate exterior held within its walls, but I never paid attention to the details.

Jenifer informed me that our ancestors helped establish St. Joseph's in 1868. The family names, Woller and Ripps, are etched in the stained-glass windows that were imported from Germany and installed in 1902. I found this meaningful because of my faith and work in the local church. I felt like I had roots. Crazy to think I might have never known if Jenifer hadn't taken the time to do some family history research. I'm thankful she's gifted in that area. She gives credit to Great-Uncle Ferdie because he passed his research on to her.

St. Joseph's Parish, downtown San Antonio, Texas

Often we value the wrong things until it's too late. Enjoy the moments and the people in those moments. The best gifts don't come in packages. "Enjoy what you have rather than desiring what you don't have. Just dreaming about nice things is meaningless—like chasing the wind."[38] You can't take physical belongings with you when you're gone, but you can receive the blessing of giving. The gifts we have are an expression of love. They were given in love and we should give them away in love. You can't give away what you don't know you have. You must fully receive what you've been given. Just like an archeologist digs up what is already there, you need to dig deep. It's all there. Be thankful for the people, things, and talents you've been blessed with in your life. Let gratitude flow from your heart, and your heart will always be full.

Being thankful starts with humility. Grandma was a confident, strong woman, but she was also humble. Humility doesn't mean weakness. It means knowing your strength doesn't come from you. Grandma knew her strength was from God.

Peace begins with humility and contentment. I asked Grandma once to tell of someone she envied and why. She asserted that she never had this feeling. Talk about contentment!

We lack nothing with Christ in us. There is wisdom that God promised to those who follow Him. We have access to this wisdom through His Word, by His Spirit. "Submit to God, and you will have peace. Then things will go well for you. Listen to His instructions, and store them in your heart. If you return to the Almighty, you will be restored—so clean up your life. If you give up your lust for money and throw your precious gold into the river, the Almighty himself will be your treasure. He will be your precious silver!"[39]

At ninety-plus years old, Grandma was still repurposing everything she could. She used the perfume samples that came in the mail to scent her closet. Grandma was the queen of recycling jars and butter tubs. She has always kept a stash right on the counter to quickly put away leftovers or send you home with a goody bag. As children, Jenifer and I would play dress-up in Grandma's jewelry and those tutu scarves. Her jewelry was always neatly sorted in her dresser drawer in recycled egg crates. I don't think she has ever owned a piece of Tupperware. She has always kept her dried cereal in a recycled gallon glass jar. Grandma's resourcefulness came at an early age.

> *In the winter, when grazing was no longer available, we burned the thorns off cacti and would feed it to the cattle. Cotton Gins gave us their hulls, and we bought a rich, yellow meal to coat it. This meal came in bright-colored cloth sacks. One of the prettiest dresses I made was from these sacks. Nothing was ever wasted. Recycling is a good start but falls very short. Things are piled but never used.*

It baffles me that Grandma lived for so long without the modern conveniences we so often take for granted. It's heartbreaking that people still live without running water. We see this, not just in other nations, but with our growing homeless population. If your home is bursting at the seams, or you have a storage building filled with things someone else could use, I challenge you to start giving it away. Look for the need and fill it. Your belongings should be your treasures. Think about what you're leaving behind—the things someone will sift through after you're no longer here. What do your belongings say about what you valued? "You have succeeded in life when all you really want is only what you really need."[40]

Sometimes we want what we can't have. Sometimes we want what we don't need. Determining the difference between a need and a want is simple: determine the problem you're trying to solve, then see if what you have solves the problem. Grandma gives us a good example in this story she told on more than one occasion:

I must tell of a time during the Depression. Mother was talking about what she would fix for dinner. We always ate at the table together as a family. Mother was contemplating a pot of vegetable soup or potato soup, which didn't seem very appetizing to my brother, Lawrence, or his friend, Raymond Knappick. They went to our grandfather Anton Ripps's[41] lake, which was forbidden to all, for it was leased to sportsmen, lawyers, and doctors for duck hunting. They brought back a great duck. It didn't please Mother, and she made them promise never to go again. Of course, she could not let the duck go to waste. I remember the wonderful meal we had with the forbidden bird.

What was the problem? Dinner. They had ingredients to make dinner, but the guys didn't want what they had, so they took the matter into their own hands. How often do we do this? Probably more than we'd like to admit.

Remember when Walmart was first trying to take over the retail world? They would allow you to return anything, no questions asked. Well, once I attempted to exchange some gifts I'd received, and it turned out that their policy had changed.

A few years back, my Christmas list was full of books! Well, it is every year, but that particular year, my sweet husband surprised me with a Kindle. Immediately, I purchased several books from my list to try it out. Later that day, we celebrated Christmas with extended family. My dear aunt gifted me the hardback versions of the same books! I told her what I had done. She acknowledged that she bought the books at Walmart, and I could return them. I figured I would get a gift card I could use to buy more books on my Kindle.

I was so excited about my new toy, until I went to Walmart. Apparently, they don't process returns for books because you might have read them. It was the day after Christmas; I don't read that fast! I explained to the woman what had happened. I hadn't even cracked open the books. They were in perfect condition! She alleged that it was store policy. I asked for the manager. While I waited for the manager, I read the store policy on the sign behind the counter. It didn't say a thing about books. When the manager arrived, I explained again what had happened. When she started to spout off about store policy, I pointed to the sign. I ended up getting store credit, but I had to work for it.

A few years later, I found myself again at the counter with a gift I was trying to return. It was a small appliance I couldn't figure out. The clerk started the return and then snarled, "Oh, I'm sorry, you can't return this because it costs too much." Their policy had changed again! The woman told me they couldn't return it because it was over fifty dollars. I guess I wasn't up for the fight that day. I just took my item and left. I get it. Walmart has changed their policy over the years due to the large number of fraudulent returns. I have a close friend who works in asset protection, and I'm acutely aware of the theft that goes on daily.

Jesus, however, is willing to exchange anything! Nothing is too expensive or too used! He died on the cross to exchange His life for our sin! He gladly took back my disobedience, my potty mouth, my suicidal thoughts, my selfishness, my bitterness, my divorce, my gossip . . . oh, the list is too long! The point is, it doesn't matter what we've done. He loves us enough to take us back—to give us the full refund, no questions asked! Jesus' policy never changes! He is the same today as He was two thousand years ago. His promises are the same and true for me, just as they were for the woman at the well.

Jesus crawled on the cross because our sin separates us from God. Jesus stands in that gap for us. Just like Walmart is the middleman between us and the manufacturer of those goods. Jesus chose to be our middleman. He decided to stand in the gap for us, to take the returns upon Himself, and to fully redeem our lives.

If you haven't taken all your returns—your sins—to Him, make this your time. We don't have to carry around all the returns that pile up and clutter our hearts. We can let it all go and trust the One who has already paid for our mistakes. "If you confess with your mouth that Jesus is Lord and believe in your heart that God raised Him from the dead, you will be saved."[42] The truth is, NONE of us will ever be good enough for a full exchange. The Good News is, we don't have to be! Our works don't redeem us. His policy includes loving us enough to die on our behalf, redeeming us fully with God the Father. Jesus already paid the price for the exchange. Works come in when you fully understand all that He has done for you, and you can't help but honor Him with your life.

We were created with a purpose: to love and serve one another. We need to stop looking, externally, for a magical purpose. It's not something we find or create. It's something we possess. Don't get fooled by the many cute sayings in Tweetland about finding yourself, finding your purpose, creating yourself. You were already created! While you may feel lost, you only need to be still long enough to listen to what your life is telling you. Our purpose is unfolding through our circumstances. I've read many books and blogs, and I've even taken quizzes trying to "find my purpose." I was seeking that one grand title that would define my worth. Don't be imprisoned by worldly labels. The hero, the "enough," the fulfillment we're seeking are all within us. Stop searching for answers you already have.

Wholeness comes from realizing you already have all you need. He is the answer to our problem, the healing for our pain, and the Savior for our greatest need. Our sense of belonging should come from knowing whose we are. Grandma knew *whose* she was before she knew *who* she was. She allowed God to guide her with His provision. Trust that He has you right where He wants you; if He didn't, He would move you. You belong. You have a purpose bigger than existing.

When each of my children was born, I dedicated a song to them as sort of a theme song for their lives. My son, James, was born in 1994. For his song, I selected "Hero" by Mariah Carey. "There's an answer if you reach into your soul, and you'll finally see the truth, that a hero lies in you."[43]

"One day the Pharisees asked Jesus, 'When will the Kingdom of God come?' Jesus replied, 'The Kingdom of God can't be detected by visible signs. You won't be able to say, "Here it is!" or "It's over there!" For the Kingdom of God is already among you.'"[44] When you belong to Him, you already have all you'll ever need. Stop praying for the things He already gave you on the cross, and start using them to be a witness for Him and His Kingdom. Allow the Holy Spirit to work through you.

If you're living your life directed by the Holy Spirit, there will be evidence. The Holy Spirit produces love, joy, peace, patience, kindness, goodness, faithfulness, gentleness, and self-control.[45] Stop praying for these things. They're already yours, if you fully surrender to the Holy Spirit. "Those who belong to Christ Jesus have nailed the passion and desires of their sinful nature to His cross and crucified them there. Since we are now living by the Spirit, let us follow the Spirit's leading in every part of our lives."[46]

Knowing what belongings are bringing you joy and adding to your life is a great start, but knowing Who you belong to *is* what matters. You may not feel like you belong in your circle, at your job, or even in your family. God knows where you are.

He will not forsake you, and He will use your circumstances to grow you. He has you right where you belong.

When you love what you have,
you have everything you need.
#WorthSaving

CHAPTER 8

Believe in Your Dreams

*"I've failed over and over and over again in life—
and that's why I succeed."*

~ Michael Jordan

G randma loved others through her cooking. When she
was in her nineties, she was still making grocery lists and
planning Thanksgiving dinners. Jenifer would help her shop,
or do her shopping for her, based on her list. Grandma would
plan each step of the preparations. She started cooking three
days out to make sure she could get it all done. Her health
didn't allow for her to stand on her feet for hours preparing,
and her stamina just wasn't the same as it was in her catering
days; however, that didn't keep her from her mission. She
would pull up a chair at her breakfast table and chop onions
and celery ahead of time. Relish trays were made up the day
before any event. Cornbread was baked a few days out so she
could dry it out for the dressing. She knew her limits, so she
adjusted her method, not her mission.

Don't be afraid to readjust. As you grow, so will your dreams.

When I was creatively avoiding my dream of writing for fifteen years, God was doing a mighty work in my character by building my faith and beckoning me to come closer. If it's God's will, He will see you through what He has called you to. However, sometimes, His call is a test. He wants us to be obedient to the calling, to the message, not the method. It's not about how we express His love, but that we do! For God, the desired outcome is drawing us closer to Him.

God called Abraham to sacrifice his son, Isaac. It wasn't God's will for Abraham to kill Isaac, but God leads him in that direction. Abraham, not knowing any different, took steps of faith. It was God's will to teach Abraham obedience and provision.

Sometime later, God tested Abraham's faith. "Abraham!" God called.

"Yes," he replied. "Here I am."

"Take your son, your only son—yes, Isaac, whom you love so much—and go to the land of Moriah. Go and sacrifice him as a burnt offering on one of the mountains, which I will show you."

The next morning Abraham woke up early. He saddled his donkey and took two of his servants with him, along with his son, Isaac. Then he chopped wood for a fire for a burnt offering and set out for the place God had told him about. On the third day of their journey, Abraham looked up and saw the place in the distance.

"Stay here with the donkey," Abraham told the servants. "The boy and I will travel a little farther. We will worship there, and then we will come right back."

So Abraham placed the wood for the burnt offering on Isaac's shoulders, while he himself carried the fire and the knife.

As the two of them walked on together, Isaac turned to Abraham and said, "Father?"

"Yes, my son?" Abraham replied.

"We have the fire and the wood," the boy said, "but where is the sheep for the burnt offering?"

"God will provide a sheep for the burnt offering, my son," Abraham answered. And they both walked on together.

When they arrived at the place where God had told him to go, Abraham built an altar and arranged the wood on it. Then he tied his son, Isaac, and laid him on the altar on top of the wood. And Abraham picked up the knife to kill his son as a sacrifice.

At that moment the angel of the Lord called to him from heaven, "Abraham! Abraham!"

"Yes," Abraham replied. "Here I am!"

"Don't lay a hand on the boy!" the angel said. "Do not hurt him in any way, for now, I know that you truly fear God. You have not withheld from me even your son, your only son."

Then Abraham looked up and saw a ram caught by its horns in a thicket. So he took the ram and sacrificed it as a burnt offering in place of his son.

Abraham named the place Yahweh-Yireh (which means "the Lord will provide"). To this day, people still use that name as a proverb: "On the mountain of the Lord it will be provided."

Then the angel of the Lord called again to Abraham from heaven. "This is what the Lord says: Because you have obeyed me and have not withheld even your son, your only son, I swear by my own name that I will certainly bless you. I will multiply your descendants beyond number, like the stars in the sky and the sand on the seashore. Your descendants will conquer the cities of their enemies.

And through your descendants, all the nations of the earth will be blessed—all because you have obeyed me."[47]

Thankfully, God has never asked me to kill one of my children. At times, He has prevented it! Just kidding, my kids have been good ones. They've even been accomplices in my creative avoidance. They, of course, had no idea. They were along for the adventure. One of my many creative avoidances was starting a T-shirt company called 2Shirtz. In 2012, instead of creating a list of New Year's resolutions, I started focusing on one word for the year. Each word had a specific meaning to me. It represented a story I wanted to tell myself. I wanted to create a T-shirt that had my "one word" on it. My creative wheels started to turn.

In 2013, I chose the word "enough" because I was reassuring myself that God would provide for me just as He provides for the birds. "Look at the birds. They don't plant or harvest or store food in barns, for your heavenly Father feeds them. And aren't you far more valuable to Him than they are?"[48]

As I was dreaming up a T-shirt idea for my one word, I felt like God wanted me to start a T-shirt company. I prayed about it, and God lead me to the scripture, "If you have two shirts, give one to the poor. If you have food, share it with those who are hungry."[49] At that moment, I felt with all of my being that 2Shirtz was God-breathed. I created a model similar to Toms Shoes.[50] For each T-shirt someone purchased, we would provide one for someone in need. I partnered with a local ministry that supplied clothing to the poor and disenfranchised, as well as a veterans program that provides for wounded warriors. Both would be the recipients of the donated shirts. I quickly learned all I could about the T-shirt business, setting up my pop-up shop everywhere I could. It was fun, and I was happy using my creativity to help others.

Prayers from My Journal

February 19, 2013: God, I boldly pray you would increase my desire to write, that the words would flow from my fingers. Thank you that I'm excited about 2Shirtz and all you'll do through it. We have enough because You are enough. We don't need to fill our lives with stuff; you're greater than anything we could buy or accumulate. We're enough in You. You've made us whole through Christ Jesus. Enough already! Why don't we get that You're enough? Help us to understand and trust Your Word. It's enough!

February 23, 2013: God, I feel like I'm on the verge of a spiritual breakthrough! Like, I'm about to get it! God, I'm stepping into 2Shirtz with crazy faith. I don't know all the details, but I see You at work. I see You in the connections, with my children excited about what I'm starting. I feel you propelling me into this without all the details. In the past, not knowing what's next would have been an excuse not to start. Thank you for trusting me.

February 25, 2013: Lord God, I want to change. I don't like the way I see the world. I want to see the good in it. I want to see the blessings. I want to see it from a cup-runneth-over perspective. You've blessed me beyond measure, and I want to live in that. I'm thankful for all I have and all that I am. I'm trusting You, Heavenly Father, for great things, just as Your Word tells me to. I can live with a little uncertainty if it means I'm walking by faith and not by sight. Guide my steps, Father, bless this path You've set me on. Sometimes it freaks me out, it feels like it's going so fast, but I trust You're in control. God, my vision is well beyond my resources. I've no idea how to run a T-shirt company, but I guess You're about to show me. One step at a time, one divine appointment at a time. Thank you, God, for what You've shown me so far. I pray You will continue to provide a path for 2Shirtz to bless millions.

The best part of 2Shirtz was meeting the people who were excited to give and those blessed by receiving. Serving alongside my daughter and husband at a giveaway with the "Church Under A Bridge"[51] in our local area was powerful. My daughter was only thirteen and learning about serving others in this unique way. My all-time favorite event was when we partnered with the Warrior and Family Support Center[52] in my hometown of San Antonio. As veterans ourselves, Darren and I were honored to serve these wounded warriors. So many of them were touched by the design of the giveaway shirt that read "not forgotten" in the phonetic alphabet. We were celebrating brave lives, changed by sacrifices, but not forgotten.

After meeting one of the soldiers, God brought me back to my vision of storytelling and writing. I began to realize that 2Shirtz wasn't the end, but the act of obedience God was looking for. He showed me that blessings don't always look the way we think they should. When I started 2Shirtz, I had a broad vision for the company and how we could help millions just like Toms Shoes. Then one day, shortly after serving the veterans, God just turned off my desire to be in the T-shirt business.

I was perplexed! I had no desire to set up shop or do online promotions. I pressed on because I had inventory and even went on to order some other shirts with our branding on them, trying to do things on my own. Instead of trusting God and waiting for His next move, my ego was deciding. We have to remember that sometimes God calls us to do something to move us closer to what He has for us. He may use it to introduce you to someone or an idea that you would have missed otherwise. Sometimes it's to build your confidence;

sometimes it's to show you what you don't want. God wastes nothing. He is weaving all of your experiences into the plans He has for you.

> February 18, 2014: I need to do what God leads me to do. Do my part and trust God for the rest. I need to let God be God. As I sit here pondering how I do that—how do I make a difference, how do I change lives?—God reveals it's not me, but Him. Why do I get so overwhelmed with these questions? I can't do these things apart from Him! I don't know how, but God does, and He is for me. I'm having a hard time trying to figure out which way to go with 2Shirtz. Seeing some of these other companies take off . . . well, I want to be impacting people like they are. I guess I need to find my "people." Who needs what I have to offer? I feel defeated. I know God has a plan, but I can't seem to rest in that. I need to!

I should have stopped when God took away my desire. Instead, I ended up with debt and leftover inventory. I beat myself up for a while about my decision to keep going and ordering more inventory even after I felt God saying it was time to move on. That wrong decision led to more creative avoidance. I worried about the financial burden I now had as a result of my disobedience. I knew God wouldn't want me to get into debt over something He called me to, but I didn't follow my heart. I was on this downward spiral, trying to create the ultimate backup plan. That's when I went back to college, as I shared about in chapter one.

Let's look at the verse right before my "enough" verse: "That is why I tell you not to worry about everyday life— whether you have enough food and drink, or enough clothes to wear. Isn't life more than food, and your body more than clothing?"[53] Then Jesus asks, "Can all your worries add a single moment to your life?"[54]

I could continue to beat myself up over my choices and disobedience, or I could choose to learn and move on. When I look back at my experience with 2Shirtz, the blessings overflow. I've learned valuable lessons, and I can tell myself a different story. Our obedience blesses us, even if the outcome isn't what we thought it would be. Our job is the input. God will take care of the result. Attend to your actions and let God attend to the outcome. No matter how small a step toward your goal is, it's better than a step away from it. There will always be risks. Focus on what you will gain through the process.

A mentor of mine says, "There is freedom when you follow your dreams." He's right! Dust will settle on dreams left unattended. The path to your dream is more about following a message God placed in your heart than arriving at any destination. God is already in the next step. Listen carefully, not to understand, but to respond. You might not know what you're being called to do. Just like Abraham, we have to be obedient to the call.

In 2013, I dreamt I was driving around a huge mountain and missed the curve. As my car went over the side, my thoughts raced—*Am I going to die in a fiery explosion like you see in movies with my vehicle tumbling down this mountain?* Suddenly, my heart wondered, "What if He catches me?" I felt so strongly that I was going to be all right, and then I woke up.

What if the dreams we're afraid of pursuing are going to turn out better than we could ever imagine? Instead of painting the horrible "what if" pictures in your mind, ask yourself, *What if God wants me to take this step, so He can show Himself through this?* Asking questions isn't a bad thing. It's asking the wrong questions that put you on the slide at the edge of the pit. It can be a quick drop to the bottom or a squeaky, torturous ride, like wearing shorts on a hot metal slide. Either way, it's dark and lonely in the pit. Avoid it!

God tells us to ask, seek, and knock. He is referring to our prayer life, not our doubting life. He reminds us that He wants to give us good gifts. Ask for them! Crazy, bold prayers beget crazy, bold miracles. If you don't go after what you want in life, you will most likely never end up with it. If you *do* go after it and it's *not* God's plan, He will redirect you. Either way, He's got you. Proverbs 16:1 reminds us, "We can make our own plans, but the Lord gives the right answer."

If we want our dreams to come true, we have to wake up. Keep doing what God told you to do until He tells you to do something different. Don't be afraid to dream. Even Joseph's brothers mocked him, "Here comes the dreamer!"[55] They plotted to kill him but ended up selling him into slavery. Not even that stopped the dream God had planted in Joseph's heart. Joseph's success later saved his brothers from starving to death! You never know how God is going to use your dreams.

Let's go back to the place for a moment where you could dream without limits. Where would that be for you? I would find myself dancing in my driveway, like I so freely danced as a child. I would set up my boombox on the trunk of Mom's car, pop in my favorite cassette, and move. I'd spin, leap, and dream. I've driven by my childhood home many times, even by Grandma's old house, my summer home. I just wanted to feel again what it was like to be so free and innocent. And to remind myself that that's what God wants for me now. He has freed me by paying the price for my sin, and He has set my heart free.

To use your gift well, you have to be aligned with God—the One who created it. To live out your dreams, you must draw close to the One who gave them to you. We already have the ability to do what He has gifted us to do. Now we need to be faithful in the little things and allow Him to multiply our efforts.

God created you. He has not forgotten the plans He has for you. You're good enough to accomplish them because He makes it so. Too often we search for our calling. We think it's a career path we take or some epic dream. In reality, we should look at the default of our soul. What is the thing we default to in a time of crisis or when we gather with others? Your calling is how your soul expresses itself. We hear God when we utilize the gifts and abilities He has given us. We understand our true self when we actively pursue Him.

Grandma expressed herself through cooking. She found great fulfillment in serving others. While I still love to dance, I realize that my ability to get the attention of others has a higher purpose. God wants to use my boldness to empower others.

God doesn't give you a dream to match your budget. He's not checking your bank account. He's testing your faith. God is cheering for you. He is the only one who knows the dream in your heart better than you do. In writing this book, I want to prove how God can use a simple girl—with an associate's degree in nothing but a master's degree in how God, the Master, works through people. I want to show my children that dreams do come true. I want to show anyone who ever doubted my wild ideas and adventurous spirit that God always had a plan. We need to focus more on the Dream-giver and less on the dream.

Judas was part of God's plan from the beginning. God knows our failures before they ever happen. He can work them into His plan for us. "And we know that God causes everything to work together for the good of those who love God and are called according to His purpose for them."[56] In Romans 8:37, He reminds us that we're already victorious, more than conquerors. These verses should give you hope. He is going to work it all out for us if we continue to be obedient and listen to His calling on our lives.

In the first year after Grandma's passing, I had three enchanting dreams about her. In the first dream, she was walking up the sidewalk of my childhood home with a box from Bill Miller Bar-B-Q. She was dressed beautifully, carrying her black purse over her shoulder.

The second dream I had about her, she was inside a roped-off display at a museum, posing like Vanna White,[57] showcasing a green tractor, supposedly my grandpa's. She was radiant in a beautiful, purplish evening gown.

After asking Grandma to show up in a dream because I wanted to see her again, God provided a third time. The first part of the dream, we were having a garage sale, and someone didn't pay for some of the items they picked up. Grandma swatted her hand through the air, like she'd done so many times in conversations, and commented, "They must have needed those items and look at all I still have." The second part of the dream, she was in bed in what looked like a nursing home, but it wasn't like the assisted-living place she lived. A priest came in to pray with her. He proclaimed to the entire room, "Be sure to pray, and when you do, do it in Jesus' name." Grandma wagged her finger at me as if she were saying, "Are you listening?"

Dreams are sacred. Whether you're daydreaming of your future or you're sound asleep, your dreams are personal. The three dreams about Grandma can be interpreted in many ways. They're very personal to me. I've shared them with Jenifer and Mom. Of course, now I've shared them with you, but your interpretation will likely be very different from mine. When God gives you a dream, don't leave it up to the world to interpret how you should act on it. God's plans for us are greater than any idea we could come up with on our own. Let Him shine through your vision.

Abiding in God is abiding in possibilities. You might find the thing you thought you were supposed to be doing was just a step to get you to the real thing. Don't be afraid to readjust. Nothing is a substitute for experience. Be brave! Go for it! Dreams are what legacies are made of. Remember, however, it's not about being busy, but being fruitful. As believers, we should be less concerned with how much we're getting done and more concerned about what we're doing. Fruit comes from the Spirit. When we abide in God, and His Spirit abides in us, fruit will be the result.

Abiding in God is abiding in possibilities.
#WorthSaving

CHAPTER 9

Bloom in Relationships

"Try not to become a person of success but a person of value."

~ Anonymous

When you discover the Divine within yourself, you connect deeper with others, as you know it's also in them. Life comes to us on its way to someone else. What God says to us, He wants to speak through us. Don't make it so hard for God to use you. We need to be aware that God's message to us is often for the benefit of someone else. My purpose is to love and serve the people I'm entrusted with, no matter if it's for a moment in the grocery store or a lifetime loving a child. People will come and go along your journey. Learn from them, teach them, and love them while you can.

Time marches on. I must tell of the journey I shared for over fifty-five years with a hard-working, ambitious, caring man. Ross served in the Merchant Marines Coast Guard in World War II. He loved sailing. He took any position to be able to sign on to a ship. His first position was as a mess boy working in the kitchen. He worked his way through many posts: he loved serving in the engine room on many trips, on tankers with supplies for the boys at the front of the war in Europe, and later in Japan, backing up the boys of D-Day with supplies.

Ross M. Hargus

Ross often spoke of how blessed he considered himself. Once, in a group of twelve or more ships with supplies in the East, submarine-launched missiles hit their fleet. Only a few were saved, including his ship. He also worked in England at what was known as Station X repairing planes. I didn't know him then. His family moved from Taft, Texas, to work at Kelly Field. We met after the war.

I moved to town when I was twenty-one. The Knappicks were a kind couple; they helped me to know I was entitled to make my own life, and my mother would get by without me to help. I was working two jobs: Mr. Wong's Grocery and the cheese plant, where we sold our milk. I learned to test the milk samples for butterfat. Farmers were paid by the amount of butterfat. For a time, I also picked up scraps for pig feed.

Grandma, age 21, at Medina Dam

Grandma—not sure whose cars these were!

There were about five small restaurants in a district where the "ladies of the night" did business. It was called the green- or red-light district, I guess because anything goes. The ladies would appeal to me to get out of the area because I would slow their business being seen. The district was just south of the great marketplace [Market Square].

Later, I was an assistant manager at the Pig Stand, and a large garage was across the street. Joe Guest, the son of the owner of the garage, went to school near there and stopped in the restaurant after school for a soda. Ross began working at the garage. I saw him coming in the restaurant and thought he was very good-looking. One day, I asked Joe about him. He revealed he had known Ross for many years and that Ross was not married. Joe couldn't wait to get back and tell Ross I was asking about him.

On my way home, I passed the garage. Ross came out to deliver a repaired car and offered me a ride. I told him I only lived in the next corner house. Later that night, he came knocking on my door and asked if I would go with him to see a friend across town. That did it! We hit it off and became friends. We went dancing on many of our dates. Ross was a good dancer.

We dated about ten months before we married on July 12, 1947, at a small church my landlord belonged to near where we lived. Ross's mother had a cake made and served punch. My mother's two brothers were there, along with Ross's parents and many of our friends. It was a lovely time for us both. We then moved in with a friend and his wife for three months until we had our apartment. It was a kitchen and bedroom, with a bathroom built in the garage. There was no hot water. We heated water on the stove. There were only a sink and a commode. It was forty dollars per month. That was all we could afford. I was no longer working, and Ross owned his dump truck, so our income varied. We married after the war ended, so he no longer sailed.

In my time and day, I thought all girls were meant to marry and have children. I think the boys knew they were to support and care for their families. Our children,

Joe and Cindy, were born in San Antonio at Santa Rosa Hospital. Joe was named after Joseph L. A. Hargus, Ross's father. For many years, Grandpa Joe Hargus managed Taft farms [Taft Ranch] in Taft, Texas—owned by President Taft's family. Cynthia Ann was named after Ross's grandma. No one was in the delivery room except the doctor and a nurse. Many women had their children at home, some with a doctor and some with a midwife. It seemed there was less death for mothers and babies than today; however, I had two miscarriages between my two kids. When my daughter was three, I had to have a hysterectomy. I was disappointed, for I loved my children. When they were babies, I made all of their baby food. It was the only way. Cereals, soups, and canned baby food came along later.

My children taught me to be more patient and less independent. When your children are born, you think they are going to be President. When they start school, you think they could be doctors or lawyers. In middle school, you hope they make it to college. By high school, you hope they will graduate. As they near adulthood, you hope they don't become drug addicts or get pregnant. When they are adults, you're just glad they made it to adulthood and that most of these things didn't happen, so you thank God. Raising children was much easier in my day. Now, they are given too much, see way too much on television, and are exposed to many evils at an early age.

After we were married, I got a Poll Tax to vote. My thoughts leaned to the Republican plans. [Harry S. Truman running against Thomas E. Dewey would have been her first presidential election to vote in.]

Ross went to work for a large construction company, H. B. Zachry, [whose work spanned] roads to military bases all over Texas, Oklahoma, and New Mexico. Many times, all the men's families traveled to areas with their

*husbands. We became a close-knit group together with our
children and had many fun times. Some jobs lasted more
than a year, so the children went to the school wherever
we were. It was the 1950s to mid 1960s. The children
were small. This era was my favorite time in life. Ross
was making a good salary, and we were very happy with
our friends and family.*

*Once, he worked for an American company mining
in Old Mexico [the country of Mexico]; he also spoke
Spanish on the job. He was gone for a month or more
at a time. Since our children were in school, I remained
behind. Ross worked in the mines in Mexico for a couple
of years. They mined Fluorspar. It was added to aluminum
for strength. When he was gone, I lived in the upstairs
apartment of my duplex.*

*I had bought the duplex when Mama sold the farm. She
gave each of the children three thousand dollars. Lawrence
purchased a car with his. Josephine purchased a house. She
almost lost it until I redeemed it and used the money to care
for Grandma. Ferdie was still a minor. Mama bought a
small house and rented it out for him. Later, she gave it to
him. When I sold my duplex, I used the money, along with
a saved portion of my inheritance, to buy my restaurant.
So keep in mind, you must always save if you want to get
ahead, and teach your children to do so as well.*

*The mineral Ross mined was not as plentiful as they'd
hoped, so they pulled out. It was then Ross started his
company, Ross Hargus Construction. He was a well-known
contractor, doing jobs for the government. He was asked to
bid on building piggybacks in the railroad yard and was
granted the contract. In the meantime, the railroad was
having trouble keeping crews to repair lines to Laredo.
They asked him to give a bid to maintain the lines, and
he was granted the contract and a crew to go work on
spurs in small towns.*

My dad, Bobby Harris, and his youngest brother, Mike, worked for Grandpa. I remember my Uncle Mike working on the miniature train track that runs through Breckenridge Park in San Antonio. My dad says they learned from the best—a man named Leonard "Buster" Harwell. According to my dad, Buster retired from Missouri Pacific Railroad after forty-seven years and crossed paths with Grandpa. That's when Grandpa started another company, Miltrack, to handle the track laying with Buster's guidance.

I also remember riding that miniature train with Jenifer and my cousin Barbie. During our summers with Grandma, she would take us to the San Antonio Zoo and Breckenridge Park when Barbie would come to town for a visit.

Ross's first vehicle was his dump truck. I didn't have a car until we were married about nine years. I rode the bus for everything, even taking the babies to the doctor.

My advice for someone getting married . . . be sure you share the same beliefs. It's not one great honeymoon. You must enjoy the good and make the best of things that may be hard to bear at times, for they too will pass. I seem to be thinking of the serious side of the journey. I want to speak of some of the fun times. There were many. We never had a honeymoon. Long years filled with happy times was all we needed. Fishing trips, family dinners, and card games. Ross's family all smoked. We never knew of the dangers. We laughed about the smoke being so dense we hardly saw the cards. Every Sunday was a nice meal and card games.

Ross's youngest brother, Howard, was always planning something. He worked in sales for Whirlpool and traveled, so there was always something to see. He would encourage us to join them, even in Las Vegas. My first airplane trip was to join them in Las Vegas. I was fifty years old. We also traveled to Jamaica, a beautiful part of the world.

It was a four-day trip sponsored by Whirlpool. They had some extra seats, so Howard reserved them for us. Jamaica had a beautiful skyline, which seemed to meet the blue waters of the ocean, with mountains behind the seashore. Many people there were poor and lived in huts on the mountainside.

Grandpa, Grandma, Aunt Doris, and Uncle Howard

Howard loved our son and daughter. He thought our daughter was beautiful and our granddaughters so well behaved. They loved to hear him tell a tale of something he did or places he visited, for he saw the fun in everything. He and his family lived in Brownsville, in deep South Texas. It was close to the Gulf of Mexico, so we fished there a lot. Howard had a boat and knew the Port Isabel area well. He introduced Ross to Walt, the owner of the local bait stand. [We called it Walt's, but it was the Hi-way Bait Stand. Walt Schofield owned it from 1972–1989.] We bought a boat. I was very happy fishing.

Grandma with her catch at Walt's

Grandpa with his catch at Walt's

I came across an article about the bait stand: "Walt was a jovial fellow, who obviously enjoyed his work."[58] I couldn't agree more. I was just a child, less than nine years old, but I recall Walt always being happy. How will people remember you?

Before Darren and I took our family to Destin, Florida, I went home to visit Grandma. I shared with Grandma that we were getting ready to leave for the beach. I told her I was going to take all the slices of bread out of the sack, make sandwiches, and put them all back in the bag. She smiled. "Oh, the memories," she giggled. She taught me this trick when she and Grandpa would take us on those summer fishing trips.

I was surprised to read in Grandma's writings that she never did learn to swim and had a fear of the water. I guess that's why she insisted on lifejackets. Grandma recalled riding in a canoe with a girlfriend who could swim. "She would get out of the boat to swim, leaving me so scared. I could've drowned." I don't recall Grandma ever letting us get out of their boat to swim. Now I understand why.

Jenifer and I probably know the most about each other. As sisters, we've experienced many of the same events and have shared many secrets with each other. We have each other's backs. During a recent message about the disciples of Jesus, I was reminded that only John was there as Jesus was hanging on the cross. If the whole world turned against me, and I was hanging on that cross, I feel so strongly that my sister would be right there, loving me and saying, "That's my sister."

Jenifer giving me a piggyback ride

I'm aware that having a sibling is a blessing not everyone has experienced. Of course, I also know many people who would count their siblings as more of a curse. I don't take Jenifer for granted! I understand what a gem she is—a real gift in my life. We can't help but laugh when we look back on our lives and see all that God has carried us through. Remember, we know all the dirt on each other. When times get tough, we remind each other that God must have a plan for us, or He wouldn't have spared us again and again. If you don't have a sibling, let me be your sister for a moment and tell you that you're still here reading this for a reason! God has a plan for you, no matter your faith in Him. Seek deep relationships with those in your circle. It might not be easy, but it will always be worth it.

When I met Darren, I was a single mom and felt I had been through the wringer. I attended a singles group at my church, and we were discussing the qualities we were looking for in a potential spouse. The group leader encouraged us to make a list and bring it back the following week. I did. Compassion was at the top of my list. I wanted a man who genuinely cared about others. When I shared with the group, one woman questioned, "I guess you don't plan to get married again?" I was a bit taken back, but I stood my ground, knowing God would provide. His Word tells us that a husband should love his wife as Jesus loves the Church.[59] Jesus is the epitome of compassion. I wanted that kind of love.

Over smoothies after a workout with a friend, I told her I wanted a husband who would love me as Jesus does. She sighed through her smile. Around the same time, another friend was using an online matchmaking service and enjoying her dating life. The company offered a month for free, so I thought, what could it hurt? I created my profile, including my priorities: putting God first, family second, and my career third. I knew what I was looking for and wanted to weed out the duds.

About three weeks in, my pastor encouraged the congregation to change our posture as we prayed. At that time, I was attending Community Bible Church in San Antonio, Texas.[60] It's an interdenominational mega-church and doesn't have kneelers. The pastor asked, if we were physically able, to kneel on the floor facing our chairs as he led us in prayer. Most people did. Later that evening, I was in my living room, winding down before bed. I decided I would get on my knees, facing my couch, to pray. Up to that point, I was a praying woman, but I'd never really considered the posture of my prayers and the humility that our stance exemplifies. I prayed that night that Jesus would send someone to love me the way that He did.

The next day, there was a match on my online profile that sounded interesting. He didn't have a profile picture, so I was a bit concerned, but everything about this man intrigued me. He was a single father raising his daughter. *Hmm . . . sounds compassionate.* We met, and I knew he was the answer to my prayer. We married within six months of our first date. I should mention that our second date was to church.

I don't recall when, but at some point, we were talking about how we prayed before we met that God would provide a spouse. Darren shared that he had prayed, that if God provided him with a godly wife to spend his life with, he would love her like Jesus loved the Church. God is faithful! He matched our prayers and blessed us both! Funny thing, we lived five minutes apart, but God used an online dating service to connect us! God has no limits to what He can do.

I'm so thankful for Darren and his continuous support of whatever God calls me to do. He stands behind my crazy ideas and dreams, is my best friend, knows my love language, and knows I love our quality time together. We enjoy two- to four-mile evening walks around our neighborhood. We talk about anything and everything while we walk. We share dreams and about our days. We discuss our children and families. I treasure our walks.

I'll never forget one evening walk when I was sharing my heart with him. (I can even recall which house we were walking past because his response blessed me dearly.) I confessed that sometimes I feel like my crazy dreams are too much. Even I think they're outlandish! I thanked him for always supporting me. He told me that's why he loved me. He loves my adventurous, wild side. He loves that I dream big and follow God's calling. He affirmed, "That's who you are, and I love you." God paired two broken people's prayers to make an extraordinary relationship. We were not meant to be alone.

God's Word tells us that where our treasure is, our heart is.[61] God tells us that relationships are to be treasured throughout His Word, yet we put busyness and media before relationships. Jesus showed the ultimate value of relationship when He died on the cross, reconciling our relationship with God. Even while taking His last breaths, He showed compassion for His mother and His dear friend John, connecting them to care for one another. Often, we're so concerned with ourselves that we don't interact with others, in fear that our feelings will be hurt or it will take up too much of our time. "Feelings are a great servant but not a great master."[62]

You don't have to rush out after reading this book to start building new relationships. It never hurts to make new friends, but take some time to focus on the people God has already placed in your life. He has entrusted them to you for a reason. Friendships have seasons, so concentrate on your present season. Thankfully, social media allows us to stay connected with friends after we move away or circumstances take us into a new season.

In a particular season of my life, a dear friend and I were having lunch at a busy deli. We always have great, long lunches, discussing everything from our hairstyles to our families. This time, my son was with us, and we were sharing one of our family quirks. My family has a thing for music. We usually sing whatever we think the words are at the top of our lungs. That is until someone else in the family hears and points out our wrong lyrics. All three of my children have had wrong-lyrics moments. Darren has too, even though he doesn't like to admit it, and, well, I'm probably the queen of wrong lyrics.

My son and I were sharing some of our wrong lyrics and then the correct lyrics with my friend. She was cracking up with laughter, and her distinctive laugh was contagious. Then I shared my all-time silliest. I honestly thought the words were, "Just like a one-winged dove, sings a song, sounds like she's singing, *whoo, whoo, whoo.*" I even thought the name of the song was "One-Winged Dove." Well, of course, after my friend acted out what a one-winged dove would look like by flailing one arm in a flapping motion while laughing hysterically, I could see how I was mistaken. Through the hysterics and the tears, she asked, "What does a one-winged dove sound like when it's singing?" My logical answer was "*Whoo, whoo, whoo.*" I thought maybe the one-winged dove was crying out and that's what "sings a song, sounds like she's singing" meant. Our outlandish laughter caused my son to melt into the booth with embarrassment.

Okay, if you're still with me and aren't rolling on the floor laughing at me, the actual song is about a *white*-winged dove, not a one-winged dove! The name of the song has nothing to do with a dove! Having moved away years ago, I find myself missing my friend and her contagious laugh. I've only seen her a handful of times over the years, but God . . . His timing is amazing.

In Grandma's hospital room, after they told us there was nothing more they could do for her, Jenifer and I decided we'd both spend the night. In case Grandma passed during the night, neither of us would go through that alone. Jenifer went home to get us some comforts for our slumber party. I sat in silence in the room, just me and the sound of Grandma breathing. To say I was emotional would be an understatement. I cried out to God. As I was praying, He reminded me that my sweet friend with the contagious laugh worked in that very hospital. I reached out to her, and she came up to see me when she was on break. As soon as she threw her arms around me, I bawled. She was such a comfort in my moment of despair.

After I pulled myself together, we talked as if not a day had passed since we'd sat together. God had connected our hearts years before, and that day compassion flowed from hers to mine. Connections like that don't come easy. We'd been friends for eighteen years at that point. We'd had our share of ups and downs, but not even distance could separate our hearts. I'm so thankful for the compassionate people in my life. We need less comparison and more compassion in the world. It starts with us. We need to be the kind of person who sees the need, recognizes the responsibility, and actively becomes the answer.

Learn to communicate with those you care about and don't miss celebrating life with them. In a time when technological advances in communication have surpassed what we could only imagine all those years ago when Grandma didn't even own a telephone, we have no excuse for loneliness. A connection is at our fingertips. The secret is to bring that connection face to face. Some lovely author friends and I have been using video conferencing biweekly to encourage one another, to answer questions about writing and publishing, and to hold each other accountable. We're part of the same online community, but the video conference cultivated the deep connection. Seeing each other face to face in a small-group setting has moved us from acquaintances to friends.

The same can be said for small-group connections at church. So often people are quick to bash mega-churches. They say, "There is no connection, it's too big, and I get lost in the sea of people." All of those things could be true, except for the small-group model most of those mega-churches follow. Deep connections can happen in a small-group environment. When we moved to our small town, our church didn't have LifeGroups. I talked to our pastor at the time and let him know I'd be willing to lead one. Nine years later, many souls have walked into our home on Wednesday nights. The connections we've made are incredible blessings. Some of these families have stood by us through trying times and vice versa. We've prayed together and cried together.

Jesus was on to something with that small-group idea of having twelve close friends. However you make friends and build relationships, I hope your relationships lead you deeper in your walk with God and your compassion for others. After all, we're all in this together.

Life comes to us on its way to someone else.
#WorthSaving

CHAPTER 10

Breathe in Experiences

"Those who turn back, remember the ordeal. Those who persevere, remember the adventure."

~ Milo Arnold

While working on this book, I asked Grandma about including some of the not-so-nice circumstances she lived through, but she only wanted to include the good. The trials would've made for a grittier book, but I'm honoring her wishes by only including what she approved. Our trials don't define us. Grandma overcoming the trials she faced was a testament to her faith and character. It's who we are after we've walked through the valley, after we've learned the lessons, that defines us, not the trial itself.

Focusing on the trial would be like focusing on the caterpillar's experience of living in the dark cocoon or the trouble he has breaking out of it instead of focusing on the beautiful wings and strength he has gained. If we focus on the struggle, we will lose the beauty of who we've become. There is a purpose for our past, but those who live in the past limit their future.

Sharing stories across generations is valuable. It takes us back to our roots. It grounds us. It inspires us. Each experience is a story to tell. Learning the lesson gives it a happy ending.

Texas is an enormous state. Even though I've lived here my entire life, I've yet to see it all. Grandma's family first settled here from Germany in 1852. They arrived in Galveston and then traveled inland. While doing some family history research, Jenifer discovered an annual Appelt family reunion in Hallettsville, Texas, at Appelt's Hill Gun Club[63]. Appelt's Hill Hall was recently featured in the documentary *Dance Hall Days*.[64]

While I'd heard of Hallettsville, I couldn't correctly spell it with all its double consonants and didn't exactly know where it was located. Jenifer told me it was between San Antonio and Houston, just south of Interstate 10. After deciding to attend with Jenifer, I googled "Hallettsville." I briefly looked over the hotel information Jenifer provided, and off I went with my trusted global positioning system (GPS). At the time, our device still plugged into your car (as opposed to coming installed in the car or on our smartphones, like it does now). Darren and I named our GPS Olivia.

I programed Olivia and we were officially on the road. I've come to enjoy road trips after moving away from home. I appreciate all the sites and seeing the different ways people live. On this trip, I didn't feel like I knew where I was headed. I wasn't taking any familiar roads, highways, or interstates. I was going the "back way," and I was relying one-hundred percent on Olivia.

Just like I was trusting Olivia, although I couldn't see the whole map and had no idea the path that would get me to my destination, we should trust God, even when we can't see His whole plan. We should take one turn at a time, one direction—not looking too far ahead at each step, but trusting that we're following the right path. There will be many distractions along the way, maybe even some wrong turns.

There will be funny signs and even silly smells, but God will take you exactly where He programed you to be. The most accessible path to follow is the one God sets before you. Like Olivia knows the way to our destination, He knows the way to our heart's desire.

God didn't create us to have more stuff. He created us to experience life in abundance. Somehow, in our culture, we've created a "more-is-better" mentality. That's not the kind of abundance God promises. So here's the deal: if you're not using it or loving it, **get rid of it!** Here's another little secret: STOP giving people stuff that isn't useful! No one needs another knickknack to dust. Start giving gifts your friends and family can use to make their lives better. Even a gift card to a place I need to go seems like a more thoughtful gift than a knickknack I now have to find a place for and dust. I'm usually not a fan of gift cards, but I am a fan of thoughtfulness.

A birthday gift I once received and loved was a book of quotes. The giver wrote on the inside cover, "To Brenda, Because every GREAT writer needs a big book of quotes to add to their repertoire!" That was one of the most memorable gifts I've received. Why? Because the giver acknowledged me in a way that touched my heart. When the gift is meaningful, it awakens your emotions. It becomes an experience.

Jenifer is a thoughtful gift-giver. She gives such practical gifts and is always finding out what you need or could use during the year leading up to the holiday. One of my favorites from her is what I call my napping blanket. In talking about our wish lists, I mentioned I'd like to have a throw for my bed. She bought the coziest blanket in the perfect color. Now, when I take a nap, it's like I get a hug from her before I drift off to sleep. Another great gift she gave me is a light-switch flashlight. It looks like a regular wall light switch, but you can stick it anywhere with the adhesive backing. When you switch it on, it's like a flashlight. I love it because I needed it, and it fits precisely the spot I had in mind. This time we didn't talk about my need; she just figured if she loved it and could use it, so could I. She was right!

The same principle applies to our life with Jesus. The more we realize our need for Him, the more we appreciate the gift of salvation. With salvation comes the life-giving relationship. When we experience God, we can't keep Him to ourselves. We want others to experience Him too!

We adopted a "favorite things" mindset a few years back. The idea is that if you find something you love or that has made your life easier or better, why not share it with everyone on your shopping list? I've done this with everything from books I've read to Squatty Potty toilet stools. (That was a fun one!) The point of gift giving is to add joy to the receiver's life or to fill a need. It's not to cause a dilemma or chore for the recipient. Grandma always gave cash. It didn't matter what the occasion was. Some people say money is impersonal. In the past, I felt the same way, but now that I'm simplifying and focusing on my mission, I don't mind cash. But thoughtfulness still wins in my book!

You could also agree not to exchange gifts at all but to share an experience. Darren and I've been doing this for years. We prefer to make memories traveling than to give each other gifts we don't need. We've recently started doing this with our three children and their spouses too. The memories will outlast any gift we could exchange.

Grandma's family didn't exchange gifts growing up. The holiday celebrations consisted of getting together with family for a big meal and enjoying each other's company. Her love of entertainment and family games must be where I get my love for the same. Remember those poker games I mentioned earlier, where we'd serve the adults snacks and refill their drinks? We eventually grew old enough to sit in on those. Then, as a family, we started playing board games and even charades. Many of the people who've sat around Grandma's table have now passed, but those memories will live on now through my children.

I love playing games and doing puzzles as a family. While working on this book, I told Jenifer it was the last great puzzle I get to work on with Grandma—putting the pieces of her story and mine together to create one beautiful picture. Jenifer and I were talking about the timing of publishing this book. Of course, I shared that I was heartbroken that Grandma won't ever hold a copy. I can only imagine how her face would have lit up. After her passing, I commented to Jenifer that I'm not sure this would have ever gotten done if she were still here and that it's a different book now after experiencing her loss.

Before taking our family (our two older kids, their spouses, our youngest, and her best friend) to Destin, Florida, Darren had trophies made for a few of our favorite games: *Monopoly, Taboo, Chicken Foot,* and one for the "Top Chef." We played a different game each evening and alternated the cooking responsibilities. At the end of the week, we voted on the best meal for the "Top Chef" trophy. I love seeing those trophies so proudly displayed in our children's homes. At any family gathering, we can challenge each other for these trophies. I love seeing the evolution of games played in our family and the added tradition of trophies. The family is always thinking up new games we can get trophies for too. My son suggested an egg toss at Easter, so Darren had a championship ring trophy made. It was great fun! I'm the current *Monopoly* trophy holder, and Darren and I are the current *Taboo* champs, as well.

We have another object on our mantel that I consider a trophy. I call it the "Compassion Trophy." I've already mentioned that Darren is a compassionate man. He makes friends with people others don't usually give a second glance. He parks in the same parking garage several times a week for work and always chats with the toll-booth employee. Lois is a kind woman. On one of our vacations, Darren mentioned bringing a gift back for Lois. I was puzzled, but then he explained who she was and how kind she is to him. They chatted about our vacation, and he thought a small souvenir would be a kind gesture. I agreed and fell deeper in love with my compassionate man. His gesture became a habit when we travel, and then one day she returned the gesture. Darren brought home a crystal on a base. It looks like a small ice sculpture. When he asked where he should put it in our house, I was quick to reply, "On the mantel with the trophies. It's your Compassion Trophy!"

Do you remember the long-running television show *What Not to Wear?*[65] In case you've never seen it, the plot is that friends and family members nominate an ill-dressed loved one. The participant receives five thousand dollars to buy a new wardrobe, but on one condition—they'll have to bring their current wardrobe to the studio and model them for the fashion "experts." After their wardrobe is deemed unflattering or out of style, it's discarded. Then the participant is sent shopping with rules to build a new wardrobe. The experts always step in on the second day of shopping to assist. Finally, the participants are sent to hair and makeup to complete their makeover. The show ends with the participant modeling three new looks for the experts and then a big reveal to the family and friends who nominated them.

I find it interesting when the participants struggle with changing their looks. Some participants rebel against the change and spend their first day buying clothes that are against the "rules" and items that are similar to what was tossed out the day before. By the end of the program, after tears and struggle to change, the participants always seem to find a new identity and enjoy their new looks. Often times, the participant states that they never thought they could look this way.

The show makes me reflect on my style for sure. It also reminds me that we not only wear our clothes, but we wear our pasts, our emotions, our beliefs, our insecurities, and disappointments. Think about this for a moment . . . you know someone who, every time you see them, you can identify their emotional state in the first five minutes. You can almost guess their struggles. It may not be the clothes people are noticing. People see the way you carry yourself. They hear the emotions in your voice. They can see by your laugh lines or the bags under your eyes what kind of life you've had before crossing their path. You experience another person's presence and they experience yours. What type of experience are you providing? How are you showing up in the world? Don't let your previous experiences or current circumstances be the lampshade that hides your light.

I asked Grandma to tell me about a time she felt like a princess. "I was always taller than the other girls my age and wished to be shorter. I never had a weight problem until I was over seventy years old." She continued, "When I got my first perm, I thought to myself, this will make me feel pretty again." Her next thought was, "When was I ever pretty?" I always thought Grandma was a beautiful woman. Sure, she had wrinkles and age spots on the backs of her hard-working hands, but her light shone from those rosy cheeks and sparkling blue eyes.

Before her visitation, after she passed, the immediate family met to see her and have some private time. I wanted so desperately to see her all dolled up one last time. Jenifer and I had picked out one of Grandma's favorite dresses and gave as much information as we could, along with pictures, to the funeral home. When I saw her, she did look beautiful, but not like I had imagined. She was almost unrecognizable, but those hands . . .

Those strong hands got me. Memories flooded my mind. All the times she'd pat my face and tell me she loved me. I recalled the last time she and I cooked together. Her chopping onions and celery like she'd done a thousand times. She was so impressed with my trick of mixing my deviled egg ingredients in a gallon-sized ziplock bag and then snipping off the end like a pastry bag to fill the eggs. It was a tender moment for me to feel like I could impress her in the kitchen.

My dad had always pointed out to me that he and I have the same wrinkle patterns on our knuckles; my fingers look like his. When I was face to face with Grandma while she was in the hospital during her final days, I noticed something. Of all things to be thinking of, I was honored that the wrinkle patterns on my face are similar to Grandma's. She had "eleven lines" in between her eyes, and, up until that moment, I despised those same lines on my own face. We also had matching parentheses-type wrinkles that curve above our eyebrows. Tears filled my eyes as I made these connections and even more come now, knowing those were the last days I'd ever see her like that. Those wrinkles on Grandma's sweet face represented some fantastic experiences.

In 1968, the city of San Antonio, Texas, celebrated 250 years since its founding in 1718 with a six-month-long International Exposition known as "HemisFair '68." I was in management with Tommy's Catering, and we had two food stands at HemisFair. I was responsible for hiring all the help to man the stands. Our specialty was barbecue with all the fixings. It was such an enjoyable time for San Antonio.

During my years in catering, I met and served many presidents, governors, and movie stars: President and Lady Bird Johnson, and Governor John Connally and his lovely wife, Nellie. I served John Wayne when he and some of the cast from the movie Alamo *came to town. I was proud of my accomplishments, for many I was left to do on my own. I was very blessed to meet and hire many hard workers. They were fast learners and made our workdays a pleasure.*

Grandma and fellow worker

Life wasn't always rosy. There were some thorns along the way, but Grandma didn't get stuck on them. She allowed the storms to pass through her life and dealt gracefully with the aftermath. She shared about a weather storm that she lived through, and it's the perfect metaphor for how she dealt with unpleasant experiences.

I was about fifteen years old when a hurricane struck the Gulf Coast. The strong winds reached San Antonio.

144

Mother and I were milking the cows, and they became very anxious, staying close to the pen. The wind blew up the dirt, and it stung our skin. We went to the house to make breakfast. Then the house began to shake. It lifted off the foundation posts and shifted to the side about six feet. We held the stove to keep it from falling over. Thank goodness the house held together, and no one was hurt. Some posts came up through the floor, but we were all safe.

The house was shaken and moved, but their faith remained steady. When the storm passed, they assessed the damage and moved on. No need to dwell on the negative, no time to waste. Grandma tried to see the bright side of every circumstance. There was no use in worrying or wallowing. There were plenty of metaphorical storms that hit Grandma during her long life, but her faith remained steady. When storms hit you, and they will, look for the lessons that show up in your fears or failures. Look how your character is being transformed and focus on the blessings.

As a good friend reminded me, cracked pots let the light out. Sometimes it's hard to leave your past behind or set your daily emotions aside, but God calls us to do just that. He asks us to cast our cares on Him. He will carry our burdens and asks us to leave the past behind. Don't walk around wearing every mistake you've ever made on your shoulder for the world to see. Everyone makes mistakes—use yours to make a difference! What we should be wearing is a smile of peace, compassion, and encouragement. Hear me loud and clear: I understand we all have bad days! I completely understand that we all have a past, and some are much more horrific than others. But if you get stuck in the bad days, if you get stuck in the past, you're missing out on the future God has planned for you.

Life is made up of a series of experiences. Take the time to learn what each one is teaching you and how God is molding you to be more like Him. To fully experience life you have to live fully through the experiences.

Don't let your previous experiences or current circumstances be the lampshade that hides your light.
#WorthSaving

PART 3

Transform

CHAPTER 11

Expand Your Faith

"Giving up makes getting up impossible."

~ Antoinette Dickson

B elief is complex. It's easy to believe what we can see. I believe my office needs a makeover because I see chaos when I open the door. We can also believe in things we can't see. That's what faith is—believing in something you can't see. I have confidence in the brakes on my vehicle. I can't see them. I wouldn't know where to look, but I believe that when I push the brake pedal my vehicle will stop. Thankfully, it does.

What we believe about ourselves and our dreams works the same way. I believe I'm pale complexioned because I can see myself in a mirror. If mirrors didn't exist, the sun would remind me in about fifteen minutes. I also believe I'm capable of accomplishing more than I've done before. I've not always felt this way. When we don't have faith, we create stories in our heads. If I didn't have confidence in my brakes, I could start fantasizing about all the horrible accidents that could happen. I could ignore the fact that my skin is pale, hitting the beach all day with friends, but the truth would be painful.

Take a look back over your life. What have you accomplished that you once thought impossible? Think about how you felt before your accomplishment. How big was your faith then? How about after?

In 2010, I participated in a sprint triathlon: a three-hundred-meter pool swim, a fourteen-mile bike ride, followed by a 3.1-mile run. I'm not that kind of athlete. I was pushing myself to do something I had never done before. I didn't even own a bike! I borrowed one three days before the event. I didn't know if I could accomplish this goal or not. I believed in something I had not seen before. Was I scared? You bet I was! Was it hard? Duh! Remember, I'm not that kind of athlete. Not an athlete at all, to be honest.

At six o'clock on a chilly forty-five-degree morning, I lowered the top on my little red convertible and heaved my borrowed bicycle over the side, standing it on end in the back seat. Driving the winding country road with my pink windbreaker on, hood pulled tight around my freezing face, I thought, "Am I really going to do this?" I recalled the words of my friend, who was also participating for the first time. When I told her I would be transporting my bike in my convertible, she responded, "Now that's commitment!"

When I arrived in a parking lot full of cyclists airing up tires, I was partly embarrassed by my transportation method. But the other part of me felt like a renegade. Pretending I knew what I was doing, I checked my tires. I quickly gave myself away when I had to borrow an air pump from the two gentlemen next to me to air up my low front tire.

I felt a bit intimidated but walked confidently to the check-in area. An elderly woman wrote with a jumbo, black permanent marker as big as she could "299" down my left shoulder and again down my left calf. I questioned to myself, "This is what they mark us with?" Feeling official with my race number "tatted" on, I walked my bike through inspection, where a buff young man pumped the brakes a few times. He then pointed me to what they call "transition." This is the staging area where you change gear for each leg of the race. Hundreds of bikes hung across metal racks in the empty parking lot like fruit on trees in an orchard.

I spread a beach towel on the ground under my hanging bike to define my space. I carefully laid out the items I would need for each leg of the race:

swim cap
goggles
padded bike shorts
cycling top with my number pinned to the front
water bottle
padded cycling gloves
sunglasses
helmet

I also had a hand towel to clean my feet after running back to the transition area after the swim. I didn't have fancy clip-in shoes for my bike since it was a loaner, just running shoes and socks. Then I laid out my baseball cap for the run, anticipating crazy hair after the swim cap and bicycle helmet.

With time to kill before the race began, my friend's family took pictures of us in front of the big triathlon banner. I tried not to be nervous, but I wondered if my weak attempt at training was going to be enough. Not a swimmer, I had only swum the three-hundred-meter distance of this race twice. That was the extent of my swim training. My cycling training wasn't much better. I had cycled four miles around my neighborhood on my mountain bike (knobby tires) a year before. Picking up my borrowed road bike (narrow, smooth tires) the Wednesday before this Saturday race, I tested out the fit for a few miles around the neighborhood. After falling over while trying to answer my cell phone and forgetting my feet were in the pedal straps, I figured that was enough training. Those few miles were such a breeze. I felt like a child riding downhill with the wind in my face. How much harder could fourteen miles be?

I was about to find out. After the pre-race pep talk and rules meeting, the participants lined up by number. Your number reflects your estimated swim completion time. Some triathlons are pool swims and some open water (lakes, oceans). I thought the pool swim would be more relaxed because everyone entered the pool a few seconds apart, one after another. I estimated my completion time high so I could start at the end of the line. I didn't want people trying to swim by me. Turns out, I wasn't last.

It's probably a good thing I didn't actually see a pool swim like this before I signed up for it. Since I had 298 people ahead of me, including my friend, I was able to see how this worked. People were swimming right past others, some right over the shoulder of the other person. I quickly found the race producer, a charming old guy named Jack, and begged to be put last. He reminded me of the rule, "Everyone will start in proper number sequence, no matter what." He assured me it would be fine.

When I was next in line, Jack was by my side, affirming that I could do this. How exactly he knew that, I still don't know. I slipped into the pool and swam to the other side. I was panicked. My heart was racing so fast I could hear it in my ears under the water. I clung to the side of the pool, telling others to swim past me. Fortunately for me, my extensive training was in the same pool. "Just swim," I told myself. I had done this two times before. I could do it now. Swimming a lap at a time, clinging to the side in between, most of the competitors passed me before I made it to the exit stairs. Climbing those metal stairs, gravity quickly reminded me that this was only the beginning.

Attempting to run, I dripped my way to the transition area. It was easy to find my bike, as there were only a few still hanging. I dried my feet, slipped on my bicycle shorts, top, socks, and running shoes and snapped on my helmet. Hopping on my bike and riding out of the transition area, I was flushed with panic yet again. My front tire was completely flat! I circled back around, frantically looking for a pump. Thankfully, one of the spotters in the area offered to change the tire for me because I had NO idea how to!

I was grateful I had a spare and that this happened in the transition area, not along the fourteen miles! Since it was the front tire, it could have been disastrous! As my friend's family looked on with desperation on their faces, I repeatedly thanked the man for changing the tire, and I watched the last cyclist leave the transition area. I encouraged myself, "Well, at least you won't have anyone to crash into." Before the race, I was nervous about riding so close to other riders. God took care of that detail in an unexpected way. It was me and the police cruiser following me, which signified that I was the LAST rider.

A few miles in, I tried to relax and take in the scenery. Looking around, I spotted a llama, of all animals. I felt exotic riding down the highway on a bicycle with llamas in the field next to me. I coasted down the next hill and embraced the moment. Exiting the highway, down yet another hill, I turned under the overpass. No longer feeling exotic but very ordinary, I pushed my jelly legs around those pedals up the hill and back onto the highway.

When I made it to *what I thought* was the top of the hill, the police officer following me seemed closer than before. It was as if I could feel the heat from the engine of his car! Before the race, they told us if the officials didn't think you could finish or complete the race in a reasonable time they would pull you out. I stopped, remembering to take my feet out of the pedal straps this time. The officer stopped. I sipped from my water bottle. Slowly, I turned around to see if he was getting out of the car. He stuck his head out the window to ask if I was okay. Out of breath, I nodded yes and managed to put the words together, "Are you pulling me from the race?" Looking surprised, he asked me when I started my pool swim. "About an hour after the race started," I shouted. After all, I was number 299. He verified that I was okay to continue if I wanted to. I told him I would, took a deep breath, and pedaled on.

Stopping again a few moments later at the *real* top of the hill, I wondered if I could finish. With my legs shaking, I took another quick sip of water and pressed on. Finally, relief— another downhill! I was off the highway and back onto the flat road toward the transition area.

Relaxed, knowing it was almost over, I was again taking in the scenery when I spotted Darren parked along the route. He had been at work and unable to see the start of the race. (Probably a good thing.) Energized by my personal fan club, I began pedaling a bit faster as I rounded the corner back into the transition area where Jack was waiting. He cheered me on as I rushed to hang my bike and change from helmet to cap. When I hopped off the bike, my legs were like silly putty melting into the carpet. Jack shouted, "Run!" So I did.

I had previously completed two half marathons, so I thought I had this running part in the bag. Never did I consider the beating I would take in the swimming and cycling legs. I was exhausted. I had cramps in muscles I didn't even know I had. The 3.1 miles was an out-and-back run. You'd run to the halfway point and then back again. I began passing runners who were coming to the finish. Oddly, it gave me hope that this was almost over. When I finally arrived at the turn-around point, there was a truck parked with one lone traffic cone in the middle of the road. As I circled around the cone, each step felt like a thousand. Shortly after, the truck passed me; there was a man in the back, leaning over and picking up all the cones marking the course. I laughed to myself and thought, "I hope I can find the finish line!"

As I made my way through the park toward the finish line, I wondered if anyone would still be there. Rounding the last corner, I found Darren, my friend, her family, and two women with the timing mat, wondering if I was ever coming back. They cheered. I cried. Exhausted, elated, and overwhelmed, I crossed the big black mat that marked my time by the chip attached to my shoe. I completed what I never thought I could do.

I headed back to the transition area to get the only bike still hanging on the rack and gather the rest of my things. Again, I heaved the bike into the back seat of my convertible. By this time, it was sunny and warm. Driving home on my little country road, I felt like a different person than I had just hours before. Through the wind blowing my ponytail straight up and the radio blaring, I heard a loud pop behind me. With one hand on the wheel, I reached back with the other to feel the front tire on the bike. I shook my head in disbelief. It was flat again! Thanking God again that it didn't happen while I was pedaling away for fourteen miles, I just laughed out loud.

Always looking for the lessons in my life, I reflected on the day. With my small amount of training, I accomplished my goal of precisely two hours and thirty minutes. Imagine if I had better prepared. We're capable of much more than we think we are. Now, if I had never done that triathlon, what would it matter? It didn't shoot me to superstar status. I didn't make the Wheaties box. I didn't even get a participation medal. What I received was much more profound. I accomplished a goal. I saw what is possible when we act on faith. In fact, just writing this gets me all fired up! It still blows my mind to this day. If I had never done the triathlon, I would be beating myself up with regret. I would have never inspired anyone. No lessons would have been learned. No funny stories would be told. My heart would be filled with sorrow. My dream would have died.

If you don't believe in your dreams, you begin to tear yourself down. You find ways to avoid what your heart is calling you to do. You begin to make choices based on avoidance. Decisions that can have lifelong consequences.

We build faith one small act at a time. Have patience and confidence to do the next right thing that will lead you closer to your dream. When we see God working in our lives, it stretches our belief just a little further every time. The key is acting on faith. "Just as the body is dead without breath, so also faith is dead without good works."[66] God wants us to put our faith into action. It should stretch you and take you to the "God-zone," where you're relying on Him. If we can take action within our own abilities, we get the glory. If we step out of our comfort zone and rely on God to accomplish the works through us, He gets the glory.

Is there a risk in believing? Sure, sometimes there is. Trust me when I say the benefits far outweigh the risks. This isn't an infomercial for one of those pills. You know the ones: grow your hair back but die from bleeding out of your eyeballs . . . Was that too much? Well, you know exactly what I'm talking about, and dreaming is not like that at all. Your dreams are there because they are a part of you. The side effects and risks will only grow your faith and the faith of those around you. It may be that one dream teaches you lessons to launch another. Dreams do change; however, when freed in faith, the legacy they leave can be significant.

Remember 2Shirtz, the T-shirt company I felt God calling me to start? God used the experiences of serving the communities we partnered with, along with other service projects we were involved with, to prepare my daughter Beth for what He was calling her to do. When she was only fifteen, she went on her first mission trip to New Orleans. A group of youth from our church partnered with MissionLab,[67] an organization that teaches youth what it means to be missionaries. They serve the community during the day and have speakers and worship services in the evenings.

MissionLab partnered our youth with an organization called Jesus Project to teach neighborhood kids about Jesus. After our students returned home, our church provided a time for them to recap their experience. Beth led the group of students in chants and songs in front of the entire church. I knew then that God had bigger plans she couldn't yet see. She was so radiant. Then each of the students had the opportunity to speak. Beth shared, "Salt is all over this world, covering the globe. We need to cover the globe. We need to be that salt that goes everywhere." Little did I know, God would personally call her to do just that. Six months later, my faith was expanded exponentially when He called her to travel with Amazon Outreach[68] to Brazil for a week.

> You are the salt of the earth. But what good is salt if it has lost its flavor? Can you make it salty again? It will be thrown out and trampled underfoot as worthless.[69]

Allowing my minor daughter to travel out of the country to the Amazon River took faith I didn't know I had. Many people were surprised I didn't go with her, but God didn't call me to go. God stretched Darren and me further when she announced she was going to apply for missionary school. She was only seventeen, with three mission trips under her belt, but she felt God was calling her to the ministry.

Youth With A Mission[70] is an excellent school with a campus, or base as they call it, about twenty minutes from our home. I was thrilled when she was accepted into the school. I didn't want to stand in the way of what God was doing in her life, but I was a bit hesitant about all I felt she was giving up. She began to fundraise for her tuition, as most missionaries do. The amount of money she needed wasn't necessarily the issue. Darren and I could have provided for her, but we felt that if God wanted her to attend the school, He would provide for her. We also wanted her to understand what being a full-time missionary was all about. The tuition was broken down into two phases. One part was for her local training, and the second part was for their outreach phase, both on foreign and American soil.

About a week before she was required to have the final amount to attend the training phase of school, she still needed more than half the total cost. Our pastor called to encourage her and let her know the church's local mission campaign would contribute toward her tuition. This left her needing fourteen hundred dollars. Our pastor encouraged her to press on and reiterated that, if God wanted her there, He would provide. I suggested she post on social media that if 140 people each gave only ten dollars, she would meet her goal. The money started to trickle in. Then she started gaining momentum, and within three days, she'd raised the entire fourteen hundred dollars! Each hour that went by during those three days was expanding our faith. Beth would get a notification each time a donation was made. It was so exciting to watch! Believing that either the full amount would come in or her dad and I would cover the difference, on the final day, I took her shopping to get the other supplies she would need for her adventure. She'd received so much by that point that we knew God wanted her there.

I will never forget Beth standing in the bedding aisle at Walmart. I had gone to the bathroom and was going to meet her there. When I turned to walk down the aisle, she was standing, staring at the bedding. I asked her if she found what she was looking for, and she turned to me, bawling—huge tears streaming down her face. I was freaked out and asked her what happened. She blurted, "God did it!" She received the final amount. A donor called her and asked how much she still needed. They specified that they would cover it, as long as she kept the donation anonymous. She was so touched by the love of all her donors, but that last call was meaningful. And, yes, we're still keeping it anonymous.

I'm not sure I can describe the day Darren and I dropped our baby off at her dorm. God had blessed her. Humbly, her excitement for what she was about to experience with Him radiated from every part of her being. She was in awe. So were we.

When phase two rolled around, she began fundraising for her outreach. I felt like she'd tapped out her inner circle for donations. My faith started to waver. Beth pressed on. She felt like God wanted her to be on this outreach and again went to social media and began campaigning for donations. There was a slow trickle, yet again she found herself needing fourteen hundred dollars a week before the deadline.

Darren and I again discussed covering the cost for her. We knew her heart was to partner with God to serve people. She'd worked to raise funds, and we knew she would continue to work toward her goal. We decided to wait until the deadline to see how close she came to raising the money on her own. We wanted to make sure that she wanted this as much as she thought she did. After all, this time she'd be spending five weeks in a village in the rainforest. She pressed on, and again, within three days, she'd raised the fourteen hundred dollars she needed. We were blown away.

In discussing it with Beth, she questioned, "If God can raise Jesus from the dead in three days, don't you think He can provide fourteen hundred dollars in three days?" Her faith expanded my faith. Seeing what God did in her life, and how He honored what He called her to do, only magnifies His ability to do whatever it takes to accomplish His will through me.

I'm continuously wowed by God. We should be. He chose us and loves us beyond what we could ever imagine. I love my children so much it hurts. It makes me weep to think He loves us more than that. All because we're His. My children couldn't earn my love. I love them because God entrusted them to me. They're a gift. We're His, and that is the only prerequisite. We're God's gift to the world, and He loves what He created. Your confidence shouldn't come from your gifts and talents but from the One who blessed you with such. He already gave you Jesus. Why would you doubt any other provision needed to complete His will? Our vision should be beyond our resources. Then it will reveal *His* power and be for *His* glory and not be about us.

I overcame the bad things that happened in my life through prayer and my belief in God. I always thought God solved my problems before I knew I had them. I've been blessed. If you believe in heaven and hell, you will understand what I'm about to say. We have been given a free will, but God, in His everlasting love for us, sees us through all problems and trials of life.

The enemy is ever present and after our minds and thoughts. I've experienced it with my mother, who lived a very righteous life, obeying all the rules of her religion. But as the end drew near, she was plagued by the enemy to forget her prayers. She even tore her rosary to pieces— one of the things she loved to pray but felt unworthy to continue to pray. I know as I grow tired, weary, and ill, I sometimes start to pray and thank God for my many blessings. Then my mind wanders, and I forget to pray. I find the enemy is at work harder to take over my thoughts. I guess God has a job ahead to keep me straight.

There are so many awful things that have happened to me that I don't care to write about. I do know that all things are possible to overcome, so never give up hope. God has all the solutions to our problems, and life can be wonderful if we do His will—even when we don't understand. Just let faith rule. How great thou art, God.

God wants us to put our faith into action.
#WorthSaving

CHAPTER 12

Engage New Stories

*"Very little is needed to make a happy life; it is all within yourself,
in your way of thinking."*

~ Marcus Aurelius

We all have stories. Stories that play in our heads. Stories we tell ourselves and others. Sometimes those stories are real, and sometimes they aren't. Sometimes those stories are sad tales from our past that we use to remind ourselves of our failures or bad choices. Sometimes, they are far-fetched tales that skew our sense of what is possible. We think these stories are protecting us from either making the same mistakes or biting off more than we can chew.

Think about the last thing you told yourself . . . Were you kind? Would you want to be friends with a person who spoke to you that way? We need to be our own best friend, instead of our own worst enemy. If you don't like the story you're telling yourself, be brave and change the ending. The story you tell yourself dictates your destination. If you don't like where you're going, change the story. Remember, some chapters of your life are worth rereading, but others need to be edited. You need to look deeper into the story and reframe it in a way that serves your purpose.

I see you just as you are, and you're beautiful. I know this because of Who created you. If validation only comes from doing good, we start to feel unworthy. If people only come around when there is "something" worth celebrating—i.e., graduations, weddings, or the birth of your children—it makes you feel like you're not worth celebrating. I'm here to tell you that you ARE! We don't need a special occasion to recognize how special you are. You don't either! Don't wait for that big moment in the future, when you think you will be fulfilled, happy, et cetera. We're not promised another day. We have to realize that our someday is now. This may be all we ever get. We need to enjoy the story we're living out. Your destiny awaits. Let today be your "someday."

A few years back, in my quiet time with God, I realized the stories in my mind play like a channel on the radio. I can change the station at any time. Now I practice and teach an exercise of storytelling that I call "Victory Channeling." I write down the experiences in my life where God has shown Himself in a mighty way. These are things I feel God has done for me, ways He has protected me, or instances in which I can't explain the miracle that has occurred. My Victory Channel list includes God doing the following:

- Matching my prayer with Darren's

- Rescuing me from depression

- Sparing me from a car accident on at least three occasions

- Answering a five-year ongoing prayer

- Providing when there was no provision in sight

And remember that triathlon with the flat-tire wreck He spared me from having? Yeah, that only happened by His strength. The more I'm aware of the way God loves me and looks after me, the more I see His hand at work. It then becomes second nature to switch from my Pity Party Channel to my Victory Channel. Or maybe my Doubt Channel to my Victory Channel. I can remind myself of what God has done for me before and that, if it's His will, He will do it again. His ways are higher. I can flip the switch in my mind and focus on the victories. God wants us to remember what He has done for us and who He is.

There are many accounts throughout scripture of people who built memorials to commemorate what God had done for them.

> We will use these stones to build a memorial. In the future, your children will ask you, What do these stones mean? Then you can tell them, 'They remind us that the Jordan River stopped flowing when the Ark of the Lord's Covenant went across.' These stones will stand as a memorial among the people of Israel forever.[71]

Isaiah 30:8 tells us, "Now go and write down these words. Write them in a book. They will stand until the end of time as a witness." While I don't build physical memorials, I do jot down moments I consider victories. Our family also hangs pictures in our home from our vacations and momentous occasions to remind us of the blessings in our life.

Throughout scripture, God reminds us of who He is.

> I am the Lord, your Holy One, Israel's Creator and King. I am the Lord, who opened a way through the waters, making a dry path through the sea. I called forth the mighty army of Egypt with all its chariots and horses. I drew them beneath the waves, and they drowned, their

lives snuffed out like a smoldering candlewick. But forget all that—it was nothing compared to what I am going to do. For I'm about to do something new. See, I've already begun! Do you see it? I will make a pathway through the wilderness.[72]

He is reminding us of His power and of what He has already done for those before us. We need to do the same thing in our lives. Remind yourself often about what He has done for you, and the power He has to do it again. Remembering what He has done in our lives allows us to tell others about our faith. We can expand our faith and the faith of others when we recount the mighty work God does. "I will praise you, Lord, with all my heart. I will tell of all the marvelous things you have done."[73]

I had the great pleasure of hearing author Dr. Brené Brown speak at a conference. She described the stories we tell ourselves. Sometimes we get in over our heads or get ahead of ourselves based solely on the story that we're telling ourselves.

For example, many years ago, our former pastor was looking for a way to raise money for a building campaign. The small group I'm a part of came up with the idea to host a church-wide garage sale. We had held a garage sale in the past to raise money for youth mission trips and had much success. Plus, we had plenty of things at the church we needed to part with, considering the recent renovations. When I suggested the idea to the former pastor, he turned it down. He explained that he didn't like the idea of asking the public to fund our building campaign. I tried to explain to him that we were only asking the public to buy items at our garage sale. We saw things differently, but I respected his leadership. A few months later, an email was sent out stating that they were collecting items for the church-wide garage sale. He had placed someone else in charge of the task, and I was offended. I was also partly relieved. I didn't want the responsibility of hosting a church-wide garage sale based on the size of the task alone. I did, however, think it was a great idea, especially since my group came up with it.

I began telling myself a story that went something like this . . . *He didn't ask me because he doesn't believe in my leadership skills. He doesn't like me. He doesn't like my idea or that the idea came from my group.* I began telling myself this crazy story, sending me down a rabbit hole I had no business going down. I held that resentment and questioned everything in my head. Fast forward: that same pastor invited me to a leadership conference. *Hello!* I should have recognized then that he saw me as a leader. He *was* welcoming and paying for me to attend a leadership conference. Then again, Does *he think I need the extra leadership training*? See how these stories get the best of us?

At this conference, we heard Dr. Brown speak on this topic of stories. Later, as we were discussing the speakers from that day, I brought up Dr. Brown's ideas about stories. I humbled myself, not knowing what to expect and knowing I had another day to spend with him at this conference. I explained to him that I had a story I was telling myself, and I wanted to know how much of it was true. When I began to tell him the story, he was shocked. He apologized that he'd been so tied up in the building campaign and designing the new building, all while continuing to pastor the church, that he didn't even remember having had that conversation with me. I believe he was sincere. I felt horrible for thinking negatively about the pastor and my perceived treatment. I also remember having so many ideas during that original phone call that it was probably overwhelming for him. I had to slow down long enough to listen and put myself in his shoes.

The story I had been telling myself was only causing me pain. He had no idea. God used this as a huge reminder to me that I needed to get the facts, communicate clearly, and not create a story. By communication, I don't mean the way we do on social media. Imagine if we communicated in person the way we do on social media, walking around, giving each other thumbs up and making faces at each other but never using words. Never speaking but just watching each other—that would be a creepy world! We can't lose the art of communication!

The story you tell yourself should take you where you want to go in life, while remaining true to your values and beliefs. Does the story speak the truth? Does the story stimulate you to take action, impacting and influencing others positively? Or is your story one-sided? Are you filling in the gaps of communication with your own doubts, fears, or insecurities? You don't have to believe you can accomplish your dreams, you just have to have faith that God can through you and take action accordingly. Is this voice in your head helping or hurting? Maybe it's time to change the channel. Often times we don't know how we feel, but we know what the truth is! We're not our emotions. We are what we believe.

Stories paint pictures. Think about the last fiction book you read or even the stories in this book. I hope they've painted a picture of what life was like for Grandma. What kind of woman she was, what kind of life she lived. Now think of the stories that you're telling yourself on a regular basis. What pictures are they creating in your head? Celebrate only the things you want to replicate. Look for the good in every situation. Sometimes we have to look beyond the present pain. Above the blanket of heavy gray clouds, the sun is still there!

We can't hide the truth. Light always finds a way out of darkness. If you're going through something not so pleasant, focus on the good in someone else's life. Just like my daughter's faith has expanded mine, let the joy of their life develop the joy in your life. Don't let the enemy use comparison as a torture device, but allow God to use it as a reminder of the good He has waiting for you! Possibilities don't end until you stop believing.

I was always too busy living to fear death. Death happened too early for many loved ones, so I learned it to be part of who we are and have faith that things would work out. It seemed I had the responsibility to see to all my loved ones' funerals—even paying for them. Keep in mind, pride is one of the great sins, so I've always remembered God has blessed me with the strength to do these things. Death teaches you that life is so very short.

I love the way Grandma told the story. The story could be tragic. It could be depressing. Many of her loved ones passed far before what we considered their time. It started with losing her father at such a young age. That could have brought Grandma to a sour place. She could've told herself the story of how pitiful it was and how she had to pay for or arrange so many funerals over the course of her life. Instead, she counted her blessings. She changed her channel. Grandma and I had many long talks about the woes in her life, but like I mentioned before, she only wanted to share the good things. Not like on social media, where everyone seems to hide behind the selfie that took ninety-nine tries to get perfect. She wasn't trying to hide anything. She just understood that her blessings far outweighed her woes. She realized that she wasn't called to share negativity in the world but to share God's continual love.

In Genesis 45:5, Joseph, after being sold into slavery by his brothers, then wrongly jailed, finds himself in a place of leadership. He says to his brothers, "But don't be upset, and don't be angry with yourselves for selling me into this place. It was God who sent me here ahead of you to preserve your lives." In verse eight, he reiterates, "So it was God who sent me here, not you! And He is the one who made me an adviser to Pharaoh—the manager of his entire palace and the governor of all Egypt."

God allowed it. God allowed those hardships to happen to Joseph. Do you think God was preparing him for greatness?

God will enable things into your life for your response, not your reaction. He was strengthening Joseph's character, teaching him about mercy and grace so that Joseph could then extend mercy and grace. Don't let others take credit for God's work. Don't let others have power over you or the mistakes you've made. We give power to everyone else's version of us. We take on the limitations placed on our potential. We judge ourselves out of our own magnificence. All we need to do is tell a different story.

I read this quote by William Shakespeare and had to disagree. He says, "We know what we are, but know not what we may be." I think it's the other way around. We have an idea of what we want to be; our problem is that we don't know who we are. We don't understand the full potential that dwells within us. If we fully embrace who we are, we'd have no problem reaching our full potential. The thing about full potential is it's unlimited.

Don't let your mind be the devil's trashcan. You're valuable, and the enemy knows it. He only goes after the jewels. Confusion is not from God. "God did not give us a spirit of fear but of power, love, and self-control."[74] The King James Version says, ". . . power, and of love and of a sound mind." We're no more victorious than the thoughts we think. Through Christ, we are more than conquerors,[75] but if we can't defeat our own minds, we're in for a long battle. If our spirit is in the right place, our mind should be sound and focused. Clear away all that needs to be trashed, focus on the treasures, and be transformed. What others think of you doesn't make it so. What your Creator created and how you act on that is what makes it so. It's time to be fully you in the story of your life.

A woman who inspires me calls herself the Accidental Icon.[76] She became a fashion icon after being discovered while entirely being herself on her way to a fashion show in New York. At over sixty-five years old, she is a fashion model and inspiration to many. People took notice of her positive spirit.

I don't know her faith beliefs, but she is fully embracing all that she is. Isn't it time you do the same?

There are lessons to learn and mistakes to avoid repeating. Part of the success of your past will be measured by what you do with it now and how well you use it to prepare for the future. The failures you once had can be transformed into success. But it depends on what you do with them in the present. We don't have to relive the story of failure. Look forward with hope, not backward with regret. Pastor Mark Batterson says, "Going back to places of spiritual significance can help us find our way forward again."[77] Notice he doesn't say anything about going back to places of regret.

We can change our channel and turn that failure into a victory. No matter what the failure, God brought you through it because you're reading this. That alone is enough victory to change the channel! Many times, I'm reminded that the very breath I breathe is a victory. My past has been speckled with near death, near accidents, and near kidnappings—to say the least. I'm sure God has a grander story for me because He spared me from so much more than the failures I beat myself up over. Some of those failures are big. Some were life-changing and have had consequences that reach far beyond me. Still, I trust that God saw me through for a reason.

I love the line from Addison Road's song "Hope Now."[78] It says, "I'm not my own, I've been carried by you all my life." When I look back, I can see His hand carrying me, protecting me, and granting me favor—long before I ever turned to follow Him. He was there. He is with you. No matter where your heart is at this moment, you're loved.

The cross was once a tool of torturous death, but Jesus transformed it into a symbol of redemption. God can certainly take our worst pain and make it our sweetest victory. Maybe you don't feel pain but resistance. If there is a limiting belief in the story you're telling yourself, it's time to tune into your victory channel. If you're at the end of your rope, your victory is that you have something to hold onto! We can always look for the positive and shift our thoughts. If you're going to tell yourself stories throughout the day, at least give them happy endings!

Many years ago, I heard Matt Chandler speak about his "Don't Cry For Me"[79] list. Matt is the lead teaching pastor of The Village Church.[80] He overcame a cancerous brain tumor. Here's what I heard:

> If you stole my computer from me . . . and you scrolled through my documents, you would find one in there called "Don't Cry For Me." And that document exists just in case I die. And what that is, is any time I have that moment, anytime there's that moment that just resonates with my soul, I go put a one sentence blurb in that document. It's about three and a half pages long now. So, it reads like this, "Don't cry for me, I've kissed a beautiful woman. (That's my wife, by the way.) Don't cry for me, I've been to India. Don't cry for me, I've been to China. Don't cry for me, I've laughed so hard I threw up. Don't cry for me, I've eaten a perfectly cooked fillet. Don't cry for me, I have great, deep friends. Don't cry for me, I've been called 'Daddy.' Don't cry for me, I've been loved." And the very last line of this document always reads the same, "Don't cry for me, I'm home."

He advised that he wanted this list read at his funeral. You may not have traveled to some of those places or done some of those specific things, but you get the point. The point is shifting our thoughts from perceived lack to a position of abundant blessings. Matt's list has been an inspiration to me over the years. When depression or whispers from the enemy start to creep in, I can always find a moment that was a victory or look for a current one. They are everywhere! If you look close enough, you will always see beauty. It surrounds us.

His list even planted a book idea in my heart! As a survivor of depression, it's important to focus on the positive things. The pit is slippery, wide, and always a step away. I'm looking forward to telling my story of surviving depression, but that is for another book. For now, know that it happens one moment at a time, one story at a time.

"Words kill, words give life; they're either poison or fruit—you choose."[81]

Thoughts are words we tell ourselves. We must choose our thoughts; thoughts kill or give life. Your story is uniquely yours. Be unique. Be authentic. We need more people being themselves. The more authentic we are, the more power we'll have. We're like sunsets, each one stunningly unique, but all from God.

Pray before you overthink. Stop filling your head with negative self-talk. You can't be who you were and become who you're meant to be. Your authenticity often gets buried beneath the sea of lies the world layers upon you. Peel back those layers, and you'll find who you were created to be. Discovering your authentic self often begins by peeling back the layers of who you're not. You're not what the world says about you or the past that's haunting you on the wrong channel. Only the Creator knows what He created. The rest is just an interpretation based on experience.

We can inspire each other. I'd love to see some of the victories that will run on your new Victory Channel. Write out a playlist for your channel. We need those victories on hand. We never know when the enemy will attack or when we will just get lazy and fall into a slump. Continually add to your victory channel as you recognize new and exciting things God is doing in your life. As you do, you will start to create a new habit of looking for the victories. Share your victory playlist using the hashtag #CelebrateToReplicate.

Only the Creator knows what He created.
#WorthSaving

CHAPTER 13

Embrace a Routine

*"And they learned, as you might, an important lesson:
clarity comes with action."*

~ Jeff Goins

N o matter your faith background, you've probably heard that God parted the Red Sea. When God was telling Moses what was going to happen, He didn't tell him, "Hold on, let me part this sea for you." Instead, He told Moses, "Lift up your staff, and stretch out your hand over the sea and divide it, that the people of Israel may go through the sea on dry ground."[82] God required Moses to act *in faith* before God did His part. We need to start operating in faith and allow God to do His part! Once we raise our staff above the sea, God will part the waters! Taking that first step in obedience is a vulnerable place. Transformation happens when you're the most fragile—you're trusting in faith and can't control what's about to take place.

Trust the process. Whether it was with this book or a new workout program, the hardest advice for me to take is to trust the process. When I started working with my publisher on this book, I had to send in a proposal that included my first full chapter, an outline of the entire book, and a chapter-by-chapter synopsis. Diligently, I worked, but I soon started to suffer from analysis paralysis. I wanted to make sure it was perfect. I struggled with everything from the subtitle to chapter titles, as well as the synopsis. I had a general idea for the book but had no idea what stories and lessons would end up here. Finally, I was talking to my publisher, and he said, "You just have to do it and know that it will likely all change. Trust the process."[83] That allowed me to be free from what felt like a commitment. Many things have changed since that proposal: the chapter titles, the subtitle, and I went from nine chapters to fifteen!

The key was trusting the process and getting to work. If I had continued to focus on perfection, this book wouldn't have been finished. We can't control the outcome, but we can control our obedience. God is asking for your contribution. Your input will become your influence. "The goal doesn't change, but the plan might."[84] Action trumps perfection every time! My goal never changed, but my plan is a work-in-progress. It's a process. Growth in any area of our life is a process.

When you're living a life according to your purpose and full of intention, your physical body responds compellingly. We're made of energy and have a unique frequency. If you were to have a heart attack, a nurse would hook you up to an EKG (electrocardiogram) to check your frequency. Similarly, they can check a person's brain waves with an EEG (electroencephalogram). The waves are our frequency. Every living thing has a frequency. Some people are naturally born with a high frequency, some a midrange, and others you wonder if they are even alive. The point is to fully live while you're alive! Life is a gift! Rip it open and get to celebrating!

Your body's frequency will fluctuate. The variables are both external and internal. Since I'm not a scientist, I won't go much further than saying that you have more influence over your body, your feelings, and emotional state than you think you do. Motion can change emotion. Action can create clarity. If you're feeling down, there are several things you can do to improve the frequency of your body. Dancing and music are two of my favorite ways to get the blood pumping and emotions in the right place. I also use essential oils, long walks, and a change of environment to improve my frequency.

Establishing a routine can be hard for someone like me with an overly creative mind. I also didn't have many rules growing up, so I don't like creating what feels like rules for myself. For many years, the word *discipline* was a dirty word. I didn't feel like I needed more discipline in my life. Setting up a routine as a work-at-home mom has never been easy for me. I've tried so many things over the years. Planners and schedules became my worst enemies. I remember the planning sessions I'd have with a friend of mine when we were both in direct sales together. We would spend hours planning but no time implementing. Neither one of us really wanted to be selling what we were selling. We wanted the outcome, but we didn't want to do the work. Planning and dreaming were fun, but since we weren't fulfilling our purpose, we weren't dedicated to doing the work. Now that I'm living a purpose-filled life, my planner is a must-have tool and not something I use to set myself up to fail.

Don't substitute what is convenient for what takes obedience. Pay attention to what you want your life to look like. Don't settle for convenience when obedience leaves a much better legacy. When you're obedient to the calling on your life, you're leveraging your God-given gifts to serve others. Paul writes in Ephesians, "With the Lord's authority, I say this: Live no longer as the Gentiles do, for they are hopelessly confused."[85] What a sad, sad way to live—hopelessly confused. We have to change our behavior if we want to change our lives. If we continue to do the same things, we will continue to get the same results. We have to determine what fulfills us to have the discipline to follow through.

Grandma always had a routine. When Jenifer and I were kids staying with her, she had our chores and errands planned out. Grandma worked well from a schedule and always kept a list of some sort: a grocery list, a list of tasks or errands, or a plan for organizing an event. She was always prepared. She also had a routine that she enjoyed. Coffee and reading the newspaper started her days, and the nightly news ended them.

After I moved away and would visit Grandma, we created our own routine. We chatted in the morning and again before bed, no matter what was in between. The day was filled with errands or company. Jenifer would often stop by after work to visit or to bring groceries. Mom would take Grandma to her appointments.

Routines can become traditions that live on long after we're gone. As a child, when Grandma would take Jenifer and me to the dentist, we always went to eat after. We would each get a shake called a Frosty. This was the routine, but it became a tradition.

The same can be said for eating as a family at Jacala,[86] the oldest originally owned Mexican restaurant in San Antonio, Texas. I remember eating out at two places as a child. This was one of them. Many holidays were celebrated here and still are. Grandpa's parents once lived next door to the restaurant. The parking lot on the side of the building is where their house once sat. The garage was still there at the time of this writing. Mom has fond memories of playing under the pecan trees and in that garage as a child. The house was long gone by the time I came along, but it's always great to hear the stories every time we eat here.

Left to right: My son James, me, Mom, Jenifer, and Grandma at Jacala

In the book of Philippians, Paul tells us to forget the past and look forward to what lies ahead.[87] We have different thoughts and feelings about our histories. Many times, we use our past as excuses. It's important to remember that the more we hold onto, the less room we have to grasp all that God is offering. Holding onto something takes energy and strength, especially if you're white-knuckling it. Loosen your grip on the things you think you should have to make room for the things God has for you.

Right now, take a deep breath, inhaling the future and the possibilities. Exhale your past, letting go of negativity. Let go of what didn't work, what doesn't fit, and what isn't serving others. Some ships need to sail away. If our hearts are full of what-ifs, and we're longing for what could have been, we're missing what God has in store for us right now. To humbly walk with God, trusting in His plan for us, we have to let go of our past—including our mistakes. We have to stop identifying ourselves by our past mistakes or the choices we've made and start defining ourselves as children of God. We're forgiven, and God has plans for us. We need to act on those plans.

To feel the call is to explore the resistance. The more important the activity is to growing your character, the more pushback you will feel. Resistance can be painful, and pain sucks. Physical pain, emotional distress—it all sucks, but we can use it to grow our character. Pain inflicted the wrong way, or for too long, can cause death. If we choose to learn from pain, it can improve us. Just like lifting weights, the more the resistance, the more your muscles will grow. Is it painful? Yes. Does it work? Yes. Does it work overnight? No. It takes time, patience, and obedience. "The pain of reaching your goal will only last a short while. The pain of not trying will last a lifetime."[88]

We have to work out our character to grow it. Don't allow the enemy to mess with you—mess with him in your obedience to God. We can't control much in life, but we can control what we choose to do with our pain. Use it. It's harder to stay where you are than to become who you were meant to be. Learn to enjoy the process, the journey. Enjoy each day, each lesson, each relationship. Difficult roads often lead to beautiful places. The broken road is part of the adventure. We can enjoy the journey if we take a moment to realize there is still beauty along that road. God is stretching us, shaping us along the way. He is preparing you to be the person you need to be to accomplish His will. Make it an adventure. Adventures are like dancing. The purpose is to enjoy each step, not to get to a final destination. "Most people waste the best years of their life waiting for an adventure to come to them instead of going out and finding one."[89]

The world is changed by what you do, not by what you say you're going to do. Change your most self-sabotaging behavior. Stop limiting what God wants to do through you. We need to learn how to pick up our cross. We're called to sacrifice. To give up what separates us from our purpose and stay close to what is sacred. Our ego keeps us from greatness. The very treasure we seek is destroyed by selfishness and greed.

Many times I've avoided self-discipline because I didn't want to surrender to anyone or their ideas about how my life should be. The root word of *discipline* is *disciple*. To be a disciple means to be a follower. It's not wrong, it just depends on who or what you're following. We cause ourselves and others more suffering through disobedience. Disobedience is like procrastination. We often realize after we complete the task that the story we were telling ourselves about what we needed to do was much worse than the reality. If we act when we're called, instead of allowing the trash to get in the way of our true self, we will find clarity and fulfillment.

You're never a failure until you quit trying. Once you press through, you will likely have a breakthrough. It's not about what you've done but about what you're doing. It's not about being busy. Be fruitful. We need to stop glorifying busyness and start glorifying God. We bring glory to Him when we are obedient. God won't do for you what you should be doing for yourself. He's also waiting for you to do for others. You can't give away what you don't have. Accept God's grace. Like Matthew West sings, "We're never gonna change the world by standing still."[90]

In the late 1970s, we began to see a change in the working world. Ross started his own business and was doing good. Large companies were selling to foreign companies and no longer spending on public relations. Young

181

people were hearing about assistant programs. They felt no responsibility for their jobs and became careless. The change was felt in all businesses. It seemed the more government programs, the fewer people helped themselves. Products became more costly and wasteful. It seemed everyone was more selfish in their dealings. We were in the midst of a changing world.

Can we change it back is the question. It starts with us. We need to take responsibility for our actions and find fulfillment in our obedience. "Until you value yourself, you won't value your time."[91] There is no time for boredom or barriers in a world this beautiful. We need to appreciate the time we have before time makes us appreciate what we had. It won't be easy, but it will be worth it.

I pray that, by now, you realize you don't have anything left to find or hide. You are who God created you to be! All you have to do is be confident in Him and be you! His peace comes when you're walking in His will. It will blow your mind. I'm humbled that He would choose to spend time with me—sometimes quiet times, sometimes working through me—both so powerful. Establish a routine that brings you into His zone. Intentionally usher in His presence every day. Surround yourself with people who see the value of your mission and will hold you accountable.

John Maxwell, an expert on leadership, says, "People can't be agents of change unless they've gone through positive changes themselves." We have to start with ourselves. Trash what is holding you back. Start identifying the treasures in your life. Create a gratitude journal, Victory Channel, or "Don't Cry For Me" list. Acknowledging what we have helps us realize how little we need. We need to be good stewards of the blessings we've already received before we expect more. The idea of stewardship is often associated with money, but it encompasses every aspect of our life. We should give the first fruits from every part of our lives to God for His Kingdom's sake. Start with your time, we all have the same amount given to us. If God were to ask, "What did you do with what I gave you?" how does your answer feel deep in your gut? Are you too busy to serve God and others, or have you created busyness to avoid your true calling?

Create a routine that works for you and allows you to serve to your highest potential. Don't try to copy what someone else is doing. For years, I'd hear people talk about how they get up at the crack of dawn and follow the same daily routine. I'd instantly feel rebellion rising in my soul. The thought of doing the same thing over and over doesn't appeal to me! I want adventure. I want flexibility. I don't want rules and restriction. I want to stay as far away from monotonous as I can get!

Here's the secret: you have to get clear on what you're trying to accomplish with your life. If your only goal is to work and provide for your family, then great, that routine is partly established for you by your employer. I'm guessing that you're reading this book, though, because you want more. You want to discover your worth and know—deep down—that it's more than collecting the paycheck you wish were bigger. Get clear on the kind of legacy you want to leave, and that'll help you establish your daily routine. We're not talking about your fifteen minutes of fame. We're talking about how all those minutes add up over time to make a difference in your circle.

Mom has told me, on more than one occasion, that I can light up a room. That compliment makes me weep with humility. While I'm thankful for this gift, I'm not looking for my fifteen minutes of fame either. My deepest heart's desire is that I leave a bit of that light in every room I enter. I want to be a torchbearer, turning on the light in others.

In the television show *Survivor*,[92] each tribe member is given a torch that represents their life in the game. When they are voted off of the show, their flame is snuffed out. We too are given a torch. Jesus is the Light of the World. When we accept Him into our hearts, we then have the Light of Life.

I am the light of the world. Whoever follows me will not walk in darkness, but will have the light of life.[93]

We're in the game! We have the light! We can't be "voted off" or "snuffed out" if we're connected to the source of light. Remember, God's calling isn't a one-time grand experience. It's a relationship that allows us to learn, grow, and listen to the little things He is asking of us. My goal is that you feel that glow deep in your soul and that it begins to illuminate every aspect of your life until it can't be contained in you. Your purpose is to radiate the light of God. How you do that is between you and God. Ask Him; He will guide your heart. He won't just guide you to it, He will guide you *through* it. He wants to be part of your routine. He's not guiding you to a destination. He *is* the destination. He is taking you on a journey and stretching you every step of the way.

If you're reading this chapter in hopes that I will lay out a routine that will magically make your life all that you hope for, I apologize now. I can't design your routine without first knowing your gifts. There are many great books out there to help you see what works for other people. I've tried some of them. They didn't work for me. How we go about our day is as unique to each of us as our fingerprints.

I want to help you live to your fullest potential, dear one. We've set the groundwork. Trash your lies, treasure your truths, and transform your legacy! Start by asking yourself, *How am I spending my time? What kind of legacy do I want to leave?* Then, just do the next right thing.

You can't give away what you don't have.
Accept God's grace.
#WorthSaving

CHAPTER 14

Elevate Your Influence

"I figure, if a girl wants to be a legend,
she should just go ahead and be one."

~ Calamity Jane

A friend once made a comment about a woman she knew who had been married six times and wanted to a lead a Bible study. My friend hinted that it was crazy for this woman to think she was qualified. I asked her, "What if the woman came to know Christ during her sixth marriage? Did it matter if it was her sixth at that point?" I wrestled with these thoughts for a few days and was reminded of how judgmental we can be as humans. Why do we take it upon ourselves to decide if, or how, God can use someone?

Let's look for a moment at how God views us in the example from John 4 regarding the woman at the well. Jesus didn't say to her, "Well, you've been married too many times, so just go thirsty." He knew she'd been married five times and was living with a man she wasn't married to. He shared that He *is* the Living Water. After revealing what He knew about her, she left her things behind, running to tell others about who she'd just met.

Do you think the effect would have been the same if the woman had not been so broken? She was so humbled that Jesus offered her a new life that she left her belongings and ran to tell everyone. She ran to the very people who would judge her, knowing her past. I believe Jesus would offer the same to the woman my friend asked about. Maybe her desire to lead a Bible study came from a humble spirit that appreciated Jesus' forgiveness and sacrifice for her sin, and she wanted to share the Good News. God can use broken vessels. Broken vessels still hold the light. The fact is that judgment is a sin, and sin draws us away from God. If we're focusing on what we think others should or shouldn't be doing, then we're not focused on what God wants us to do.

I learned this lesson the hard way. As a new follower of Christ, I allowed myself to be influenced by what I thought was a more mature believer. When she gave me advice in a family situation, I took it. In doing so, I stood in judgment of two people I cared for and loved. At the time, I was recovering from a deep depression. I just wanted the tension in my heart to stop. I didn't understand that I was only creating more. I knew what I was doing was wrong. With every part of my soul, I knew I should love these people, not push them away. As you can imagine, many hurtful exchanges took place, and I placed judgment on two people I cared about. Looking back now, I can't believe I was that person. I was so full of myself that I took God's role upon my shoulders. It wasn't until a year and a half later that I came to fully understand the magnitude of what I'd done.

The very same, seemingly spiritual, advice-giver turned her judgment on me. I was shocked! As, I'm sure, my victims were too. I thought we had a decent relationship. I knew I didn't live up to her standards as a wife or homemaker, but the judgment and attack were so personal. She attacked my character. As Donkey would say from the movie *Shrek*,[94] she cut me deep. I was crushed that someone I looked up to would hurt me so deeply.

In discussing it with Darren I asked, "When did Jesus go on vacation and leave her in charge?" As soon as those words left my lips, I was convicted of how I was judging others. I was humbled by the pain—both the pain I felt and the pain I had caused. I felt completely misunderstood. I cried out to God, asking Him to forgive me for trying to be Him—trying to take on His role. He affirmed that I was His. He reminded me that I'm forgiven and called to love Him and others. I'm thankful for His forgiveness of my past and for the mistakes that I continue to make as I learn and grow in my relationship with Him.

God used this experience to show me how to love like He loves. We will never have enough information to judge another person—it's not our place—but we already have enough information to love them. After my eyes were opened to the pain I had caused the two individuals I so wrongly stood in judgment of, I called to apologize. The response was a blessed surprise. I was told I was forgiven and there was no need to apologize. They understood—it was just part of me growing up and finding my way. I was so humbled. It was as if God was speaking directly to my heart.

There are so many valuable lessons from that experience. We have to realize that our influence can either hurt people or it can help people. It's part of the legacy that will stay behind long after we're gone. Long after the people in that story are gone, I'll remember what transpired and how one's advice caused so much pain for many people. We must use our influence wisely and carefully.

Hurt people hurt people. Healed people heal people. Heal your heart, so you don't break others. No matter what position you hold in your job or family, whether you consider yourself a leader or not, you're influencing someone. To be broken is no reason to see all things as broken. In some ways, seeing brokenness can be beautiful. It allows you to have empathy for another person. If you're not careful, though, it can cause you to be critical. If you only recognize the broken and don't see how those pieces make up the masterpiece that you are, you're taking another step toward the slide. Use your own brokenness to help heal the brokenness you see in others. To ease the suffering of another often eases your own.

God will give you the desires of your heart,[95] scripture tells us; but we must delight in the Lord, not in ourselves. Sometimes we miss the second part of that verse. God did not create us for ourselves. He created us to be in a relationship with Him and others. It's not about us. He says the second greatest commandment is to "Love your neighbor as yourself."[96]

The only way we're going to impact and influence others is to get out of our own way and love people where they are. Love like it matters. It does! We need to love like we know the pain of not being loved. We find courage when we're loved deeply. Loving others this way gives them wings. We need to love deeper, seeing people soul to soul. When I look at you, I should be thinking, *How I can serve you?* Most often, we're considering the opposite: *What's in it for me?* If we genuinely want to influence people, we should ask ourselves, *What can I do to help this person be all they were created to be? How can I help heal their brokenness? How can the experiences I've had help this person?*

I'm not saying we should run around trying to fix everyone. We can't do that anyway. But we can indeed show love to them. We can shine a bit of light their way. Remember, some pursue happiness, others create it. Always try to leave people better than you found them. Show gratitude to others and to God. (And not necessarily in that order!) Everyone wants to be appreciated. Reach out to the people who have influenced and encouraged you. Let them know part of their heritage will be carried forward through you because of the influence they've had in your life. A legacy worth leaving is made with love.

A while back, I went to a mini conference here locally. The speaker shared how it drove her husband crazy when she left a spoon in the sink. Sometimes she would do it on purpose just to annoy him. Then she realized that she could show him that she loved him just by putting the spoon in the dishwasher. It stirred up some controversy with the women at our table. One friend was somewhat defiant about giving in to such "demands."

I piped in and explained that I make the bed at my house only because Darren likes it. It's a simple way I can show him I love and respect him. I don't like making the bed. Well, maybe I do now with my new bedding I received for Christmas, only because it looks so stinking pretty and makes me feel like I'm on vacation, but don't tell Darren. Before the new bedding, I would dread all the pillows. We have far too many. I know—first-world problems! I realize I'm blessed with even having a bed to make. I get to. That's a privilege. That is not the point here. The point is, we can show people we love them by doing the simplest acts of kindness. Why make something a battle when giving in does so much good? It feels good to make people happy.

God is much more interested in changing us than He is in improving our situation. If your circumstances aren't pleasing to you, ask yourself if God is trying to do a work in your heart. How we respond to situations influences those around us. The real question is, do you *respond* or *react*? You might not think there is much of a difference. Learning the difference could save relationships and your ability to influence others. Reacting usually happens without thinking. It's a snap decision, sometimes in opposition to a situation. Responding is answering. It's more thoughtful. Over time, you can learn how to control your reactions, as well.

First responders are taught how to manage their reactions. Emergencies are stressful, and if everyone just reacted to what they saw, it could be chaos. With the proper training, you can learn how to manage the situation in a planned or methodical way. Good leaders know the difference between responding and reacting. When things don't go your way, you may be tempted to react by quitting or by defending yourself. Great influencers take the time to respond, rather than reacting. They know that what happens next could make or break their relationships and ruin their opportunity to have a positive effect on someone's life.

Grandma knew the difference between responding and reacting. It made her a woman of influence. It started with how she embraced her circumstances. She always looked for the good and just did the next right thing. She became a cook because her circumstances put her in a situation where she felt she had to step up and help.

> *I was always adventurous growing up. I was mature beyond my years. I was active and learning everything I could, from milking cows to driving tractors. A significant turning point in my life was when I was twelve or thirteen years old. I knew I had to step up and help my mother with chores and making decisions about our lives, for no one else did.*
>
> *Everyone thought of me as a good cook. It was something I learned early and loved to do. When our son was in college and our daughter in high school, it was then I quit management and bought my restaurant and*

catering business. It grew very fast. I was able to train some outstanding people: assistant manager, head waitress, morning cook, noon cook, and many more for catering. It's such a blessing to be able to do what you love. It was just basic meals and the use of herbs and seasonings.

If you want to start a business, first learn everything you can, and enjoy what you're doing. Work hard and believe you can succeed. We seem to have lost the time for home cooking with family preparing meals and time to eat together. It seems we've lost the real meaning of family. I feel I should share some recipes. I will start with one I was very proud of and enjoyed cooking as well as eating:

(These recipes are from her memory and extensive knowledge of cooking. They may seem incomplete, but it was just second nature for her to whip something up. I'm sharing them to honor what she wrote and at the request of many family members, not necessarily to follow as written.)

Chicken Fried Steak
Take 1 or 2 beef or veal cutlets per person
Tenderize it by beating it
Dip in seasoned flour (salt and pepper)
Shake off excess
Dip in mixture of 1 cup buttermilk and whipped egg
Drain
Then press into mixture of flour and crushed french-fried
    onion
Fry in fat, and brown all sides
Serve with cream gravy

Cream Gravy
1 cup flour mixed with 2 tablespoons of oil or oleo.
Add milk and boil, stirring constantly until done.

Cornbread Dressing
Bake cornbread and let cool
Cook 1 pound crumbled sausage
Add 1 cup finely chopped onion
Add ½ cup chopped celery
Add 2 cups dry bread crumbs,
1 teaspoon sage,
1 tablespoon black pepper,
A small amount of salt
Add crumbled cornbread
Mix in 4 eggs
Add chicken broth to make the consistency mushy
Bake in 350-degree oven, about an hour to 1 ½ hours

Pot of Pinto Beans
Clean and rinse 2 cups pintos
Place in large pot and cover with 4 cups water
Add 2 cloves chopped garlic
Bring to boil
Add cooked bacon, hearty tomato, and chili sauce
Add 1 teaspoon cumin when done
Don't salt until done, so beans can get creamy

Rice Pilaf
1 cup rice cooked in chicken broth
4 green onions, cut fine with all the greens
2 carrots, chopped fine
Sauté in oleo
Add to rice

Spanish Rice
2 tablespoons cooking oil
2 cups long-grain brown rice
1 large onion, chopped
½ large bell pepper, diced

Sauté only until onions are clear
Add 8-ounce can diced tomatoes
2 cups chicken broth or water
Salt and pepper to taste
1 teaspoon cumin
Cover and simmer without stirring until all fluid is gone
    and rice is done
Enjoy
Makes 12 servings

In the years after closing my restaurant, Ross's brother, Howard, became an outfitter for hunters of white-wing doves, mostly in Mexico. He was in need of someone to prepare the meals for the hunters, so I went with him and cooked for over four months a year and enjoyed it. We spent part of July getting ready. August, September, and October were hunting season, and we spent part of November closing up camp. Ross came down to join us and hunt on weekends. It was like a vacation for us all.

Ross on a hunting trip

The remainder of the year, I cooked and managed the kitchen for the local club. In fact, the secretary of the club suggested I attend a meeting for a health maintenance organization (HMO), since I was retiring. We joined, and I've been taken care of—all my medical needs, including the supervision of a fine doctor and referrals to grand specialists.

Your work is the footprint you leave on this planet. Not your job, but your life's work. Grandma's life work was loving people through her gift of cooking. She did this in various positions throughout her life. The title didn't matter. If she was cooking and serving others, she was content. We should work to make an impact, not to get a better title. If you're feeling the imposter syndrome, you need to stop saying, "I'm not worthy of this title, position, or gift because of my family background, education, et cetera." You're worthy because you were called!

Our power and strength come from our Source. I call Him God, my Creator. We can harvest energy from our pasts, our families, and our dysfunctions by leaning in to the lessons we learn, but we must stay plugged into our Source to convert that power to fuel. Your electronics won't be very powerful if they aren't charged regularly. A cup of the ocean doesn't have the same power as *the* ocean. It has been separated from its source. We must stay connected to our power Source.

Someone is waiting for you to use your gifts. Let your gifts become a gift to others. It's not about you, but who you can serve. Someone is waiting for your help and your kindness. Your circle needs someone awakened to their potential to show them the way. It's not about who sees you but who you're seeing, serving, and sacrificing for. Maximize what you've been given. Their future help depends on your present courage. Love people to love them, not to be loved in return. Seek to be worth knowing rather than to be well-known. We cannot control how someone feels about us. We need to love as we have been called to do. As Ronald Reagan put it, "Live simply. Love generously. Care deeply. Speak kindly. Leave the rest to God."

In the end, we will be asked what we did with what we were given. We've been given a great love. Even if you think your time was wasted on someone else, it was not lost if you loved. The hope in my heart is bigger than the message of despair in the world. The most wasted of all days is one in which you serve no one but yourself. You possess the power to enhance the life of another. It might be complimenting the cashier at your local store, or it might be walking with someone through their faith journey, being their shoulder to cry on or their ladder holder.

Get real with God. Don't hide in your fig leaves. Run to God! Let Him cover you with His righteousness and forgiveness. He has called you to greatness. We're more than conquerors! Live and serve as the masterpiece you are! In Christ, we can find a purpose for the pain, strength for the struggle, and faith for the fight. Consume knowledge with the intent to serve others. Knowledge needs to move from your head to your heart, and from your heart to your hands. It means nothing if you hoard it. Fill up so you can pour out. "Wisdom will multiply your days and add years to your life."[97]

Honor is the currency of elevation. Servants see no differences in the people they serve, only the hearts. We're one race—the human race. There shouldn't be a competition but a stewardship. It's not about who has more or is doing more. It's about how you're leveraging what you've been given. With great blessings comes great responsibility. At the end of our life, we're going to be held accountable for our own actions, not compared to the actions of others. Our deeds should outweigh our words and intentions. Scripture says we're each given our portion according to our abilities. God knows our potential. As my friend Joan L. Turley says in her book, *Sacred*

Work in Secular Places, "He alone knows the value of what we lay at His feet and the purity of which our gift is offered."[98]

What we do consistently, not on a rare occasion, is what builds a legacy. Learn to say no to things that don't honor your purpose, time, health, and family, so you can answer yes to serving God and others. When you say yes to the right things, you build a powerful legacy.

I want the most beautiful thing about me to be my heart and my passion for others. When you see me, don't think I have it all together. I'm broken. God is the One holding the broken pieces together. It's His light you see shining through the cracks. Some of my most vulnerable thoughts have been shared in these pages. I feel like my heart has been ripped open. I've been exposed, yet I will take the risk . . . because you're worth it. I will take the chance because I have to. I braved burning the boats to touch your life. I will purge my words. I will give away a precious part of my soul that I've hoarded for so long.

Fully living is vulnerable and raw. It's risky. It's rewarding. Beautiful soul, you can do hard things. The more you do, the more you grow. Stand in your truth. Be your own hero. Then you can be a hero to others. Mark Twain proclaimed, "Great people are those who make others feel that they, too, can become great." Negative energy is sticky. Stay away from it so it won't stick to you, and don't leave a trail for others. We often hold pain from previous generations. We need to let the hurt go for our sake, but we also need to release it for the sake of those we influence.

You have a unique perspective. Don't be afraid to share it. Life is not about growing our pocketbooks, waistlines, or hair—even though I'm growing mine out again. My hair, that is! It's about stretching our characters, our souls. Maturing isn't about age but about owning the responsibilities you've been given. It's not just the responsibility of going to work and earning a paycheck to keep the lights on. While that is important, you've been called to an intricate purpose. You need to accept the grace that's been extended to you. Embrace all that you were created to be, so that you can unselfishly love and serve others. We can only ever be who we were created to be, and at some point, that has to be good enough for us to move forward in faith.

Grow, stretch yourself, and be generous with your blessings. Everything God created was meant to grow, including you. The way you feel about yourself is directly reflected in the way you treat others. People are messy, but the Cross was messier. Jesus sacrificed His life for us, and He wants us to take up our cross for others. Those who radically sow radically reap. If you speak kind words, you will hear kind echoes.

Our very existence is making an impact. Be intentional about the difference you're making. Be aware of how you're showing up in the world. Your life matters. Your presence in the room matters. If you're tired and think you'll just sit this out, you're fooling yourself. Your inaction is impacting your circle. People who make a real difference don't make a big deal out of themselves. They make a big deal out of God. They don't get in the way of what He is trying to do through them or the people He is trying to reach.

At a conference I attended in California, there were influential speakers from all over the country giving inspirational messages. At the time of the conference, I suffered from plantar fasciitis. For those of you unfamiliar with this condition, first be glad you haven't heard of it. That means you probably don't have it. It's a foot condition caused by the tightening of the muscles in your legs and the "fascia," a band of tissue in the bottom of the foot. It produces small tears in the fascia and is very painful.

During one of the first sessions at the conference, an athletic man came bouncing on the stage full of energy and life. He was a personal trainer and was encouraging us to drink water and stretch. He even led us through some stretches. He mentioned that he had helped many overcome back pain and other ailments and said to stop by to meet him if you had any questions. Well, you can bet I did. I wanted to know the magic stretch that was going to heal my feet!

Over one of the breaks, I ran into him outside the doors of the Crystal Cathedral,[99] where the conference was being held. I told him about the problem with my feet, and he was familiar with the diagnosis. He suggested a stretch that my doctor had already shown me, and I felt a bit disappointed. I was expecting the miracle cure! What I didn't expect was what happened next. This buff man in his training shoes, warm-ups, and Under Armour shirt asked what else was bothering me. I quickly replied, "Nothing. If my feet would heal, I would be great."

He saw what I couldn't. He began asking personal questions about my family and my past, and he was right about every one of them. He asked if I was from a broken home and if my dad was around. Then we began talking about some pretty significant things that had just occurred in my life. Before I knew it, I was sobbing like a baby—pouring my life out to this personal trainer. People were walking by, going into the next session, but he focused on me. The words he spoke were powerful. He was referencing scripture, God's plan for me, and he even prayed for me. I was standing there thinking, *This guy is supposed to heal my feet not my heart!* It was a divine appointment. I thank God for that moment because, through this man, a total stranger, my heart began to heal from those wounds. My feet, well, eventually I learned the magic stretches, and they're fine.

I believe when God gets a hold of us, He gives us a new name. Biblical examples would include Abram to Abraham and Saul to Paul, just to name a couple. I don't know if this man was a personal trainer before he was a Christian, but God gave a new meaning to that title. This man was using his influence to heal more than bodies. He understood his calling was helping others, and he did it in every way he could.

A few people who have had an impact on my life: of course, my mother, she was a very strong woman; the nun who taught me in school; and one of the priests who helped me through the many stressful times after my dad died. Everyone in my family had problems of their own, so I kept mine to myself.

Grandpa and Grandma Ripps lived near us. Grandma would visit with mother and speak in German. She loved to tat [handcraft lace] and knit, which was not my thing. Seems I always got in trouble in her flower garden. I once stepped on all her cacti and broke them off. Grandpa Ripps read a lot of the Bible. He never had much to say—except after my dad died. Dad left no will, so he was appointed the administrator over us kids. He seemed to think Mama would waste the estate.

My Grandmother Appelt (Dad's mom) was always so proper. When she stayed with us, she never left her room before she was fully dressed with hair combed in a bun. Grandpa Appelt, I didn't know very well. I only recall seeing him once, and he died ten months before my dad. Grandma stayed with her oldest daughter, Emma, and we didn't see much more of her.

The world was changing so fast; you felt you had to run to keep up. We went from horse and buggy, to automobile, to planes, and space—and television brought it all to our daily lives. The world was no longer the mostly unknown.

We need to let the hurt go for our sake, but we also need to release it for the sake of those we influence.
#WorthSaving

CHAPTER 15

Enhance Your Legacy

"The goal isn't to live forever. It is to create something that will."

~ Chuck Palahnuik

When did we get in such a hurry? What are we racing toward? Often when I visited Grandma, she would fuss at me for "going a hundred miles per hour"—not in my car, but in my life. She would say, "You just go, go, go." I guess to some extent I did, especially when I was visiting. I'd try to squeeze in as much time with friends and family, as well as eating at my favorite San Antonio spots—places we don't have in my small East Texas town.

It seems we're always in a hurry to get to the next thing. We hurry all week to make it to the weekend. We rush through holidays so that we can get back to a regular routine. What are we rushing toward? We think there'll be something more fulfilling around the corner, so we rush from one thing to the next. Often times, I have to remind Darren when we travel that we're on *vacation!* In my mind, that should include some rest. He's like me on my trips home, trying to cram so much into the short time we have. By the time we get home, I need a vacation from my vacation! It usually takes me a week to get caught up on rest! Don't get me wrong, I love traveling and count it as a blessing. I just want to slow down. We need time to process the things we're experiencing—both on vacation and in life.

If asked to list my many blessings, I would have to count the days I've had on this earth. Each day was a blessing, meeting each trial of life and its joys. The many joys—the births of my children, the love of my three granddaughters, and the growing number of my great-grandchildren. Much love and understanding was given to me by the many people I met along the journey.

Grandma counted her 34,037 days on earth as blessings. That's an abundance of blessings! Not to mention the other things she lists. She viewed her days as blessings because she didn't zoom through them like she was trying to set a new personal record. She'd lost so many loved ones before their time; she understood the value of each day. She counted them as blessings because she knew Who provided them: "My peace has always been my belief in God, my Creator. I know I could not reach the life I have without His love." When we take a closer look at Grandma's legacy—one of courage, faith, values, strong work ethic, love, and generosity—we can see it started with her own mother.

One of my many helps through problems was remembering my strong mother. She suffered many trials, never complained, just kept working through them and trusting in God. Never asking anything for herself, very unselfish—it's a shame it took me so long to realize this. She knew the word love *was more than a word, and she put it to work in her everyday life.*

Grandma and her mother

Love is sacrificial. It leaves powerful, positive legacies. I'm so thankful for the time I had with Grandma after she asked me to write this book. This process has been a magnifying glass for our relationship and the lessons she taught me. It also expanded the relationship I have with Jenifer. We have shared more memories, road trips, laughs, and even tears because of this project. I could say the same for my mother and children; many field trips to Mission Espada or the library included them. The process of this book has also deepened my relationship with Darren and many friends. It's amazing how obedience can open up new friendships and experiences. Grandma's glow illuminated numerous lives in her ninety-three years and is now gleaming in the lives of many more. Her legacy is brightly reflecting the Light she held so dearly.

Over the years, I've jotted down many lessons, thoughts, and memories. I've been living with this book in mind and filtering everything that happens to me through this book. The best part about life's distractions is that they are usually affirming your purpose. I stand in awe! When God put the desire in my heart to write back in 2003, I had no idea what the outcome would be. Still I don't. He can do whatever He wants. I'm surrendering it all to Him. Interestingly, my desire never wavered over the fifteen years it took to write this book. As ideas came, I jotted them down in my journals, favorite writing apps, or whatever slip of paper I could find. Even though I wasn't actively writing the book, it was writing itself.

Part of the reason I had to complete this project was for you, my reader, my friend. I don't want you to wait to fully live. Unleash your potential! You don't need to wait until next year, until things are "right," or you have it "all together" to make the transformation. You only need this moment. Take time to reflect on the cost of not accomplishing what your heart desires. My deepest desire is to help you shine your light. It's not enough that you see my light; you need to see your own. It's there. You're valuable. Your story matters. The role you play in the stories of others matters.

> You are the light of the world—like a city on a hilltop that cannot be hidden. No one lights a lamp and then puts it under a basket. Instead, a lamp is placed on a stand, where it gives light to everyone in the house. In the same way, let your good deeds shine out for all to see so that everyone will praise your heavenly Father. [100]

> *All my thoughts seem to be of the things I received from the people I've known and met. I do hope I've given something to all, meant something to them, and offered some help to each along the way. For Nat King Cole once sang, "The greatest thing you'll ever learn is just to love and be loved in return."*[101]

Jesus tells us, "Your love for one another will prove to the world that you are my disciples."[102] When you take your eyes off yourself, and trust that God has given you a moment to love those around you—for His Kingdom's sake—it changes the lenses by which we see the world. When I was younger,

I had no idea what love meant. I remember reading in God's Word for the first time,

> Love is patient and kind. Love is not jealous or boastful or proud or rude. It does not demand its own way. It is not irritable, and it keeps no record of being wronged. It does not rejoice about injustice but rejoices whenever the truth wins out. Love never gives up, never loses faith, is always hopeful, and endures through every circumstance. Prophecy and speaking in unknown languages and special knowledge will become useless. But love will last forever![103]

When you read this familiar passage, don't read it from the perceptive of what you should be getting; but, instead, insert your name where it says "love." Read it from the perspective of who *you* should be. As we worry less about whether we matter and start treating others like they positively do, we begin to see how much *we* do. "People will summarize your life in one sentence, pick it now."[104]

You only have one life. Don't hoard it for yourself. Give it to God and watch Him multiply it for eternity. We're all going to die. It's best not to wait until the end to start living. We're all created by God for a purpose. He has gifted us each uniquely. He provides everything for you to accomplish His will for your life. Stop overcomplicating His plan with doubt. Grab hold of His hand. Use the gifts He has given you to bless those around you. Daniel Webster advises, "What a man does for others, not what they do for him, gives him immortality."

Multiply God's goodness by giving away the same grace you've received. Gratefully acknowledge all He's blessed you with. We should be thankful that God always turns out to be bigger than we thought. Let your legacy be glorifying to the One who created you. Though your soul may leave earth as you meet Jesus in heaven, create a legacy that will linger like the smell of fresh-baked cookies at Christmas. Legacies are created one moment at a time. "Sometimes you will never know the value of a moment until it becomes a memory."[105]

I'm not sure if Grandma heard this somewhere, but when asked what advice she would give me, she replied, "The past is behind—learn from it. The future is ahead—prepare for it. The present is here—live it."[106]

There's more to life than waking up, going to work, and coming home, just to go and do it all again. Life is not about how much we can accumulate but how much we can give away. We must be intentional because we're influencing and impacting those around us. We can be the difference. It's not for fame or money. Your self-worth should not be connected to your net worth. "Money is fuel, you decide what to light on fire."[107]

A legacy, by definition, is an inheritance, endowment, gift, settlement or birthright. You're born with specific gifts that God created in you uniquely to share with the world. This is your birthright. You've also been blessed by the legacies of those around you and before you. Don't let money be your motivation or your limitation.

The art of upcycling is turning something into something better than it was before. Upcycling is a form of recycling, and often the items used were to be discarded or were considered waste material. In comparison, recycling is turning waste into a reusable product and, most often, a close form of the original. Reusing is merely using the item for a different purpose, just as it is. Grandma was a master of all! She reused, recycled, and upcycled—not because it was the thing to do, but it made sense to her.

Remember, Grandma grew up in a time when things were not abundant. Walmart didn't exist when she was a child.

It didn't open until July 2, 1962. Grandma was thirty-nine years old! Amazon, the Container Store, and IKEA didn't exist either. People either went without or made do with what they had. Grandma was creative. She reused egg crates as jewelry containers, perfume samples as closet and drawer fresheners, and butter tubs and jars as Tupperware.

When recycling did become a thing, Grandma recycled everything that could go in the bin. She always had a container by her chair to toss the newspaper in after she'd read it. She'd fill it so full she couldn't lift it, but anytime Jenifer or Mom would visit, they would empty it for her. They were good at keeping up with it. I only remember taking it out a couple of times myself. Grandma knew what could be recycled and what couldn't, and you'd better put the right item in the right bin! I'm sad to admit that, where I live, we currently don't have a curbside recycling program.

After hearing the title of this book, many people thought it was going to be a book about recycling and crafting with recycled butter tubs. I hope by now you realize it's just a metaphor for the way Grandma saw life. Everything had a purpose. She saw the value in the simplest things and, most importantly, in people. Grandma upcycled before the word *upcycling* even existed. She invested in people, and they became better versions of who they were before. That is precisely what I want to do! It's one thing to meet someone, have an enjoyable experience, and then leave like nothing ever happened. It's another to leave the presence of someone and be changed by their love.

Butter tubs are plastic. Plastic isn't biodegradable. It lasts forever! So will your legacy! Be intentional about loving people. Let your light shine, illuminating the lives of others until their lights shine, creating waves of radiance. The transformation of your life and legacy begins with you. Many of the memories in this book I never thought I would share with anyone. When Grandma asked me to write this, I thought, *Sure, I can type up what she wrote.* I didn't realize the treasure I'd dig up in clarifying her points and expressing her ideas. One of my favorite authors on the subject of writing says, "A calling isn't something new and shiny. Often it's something old and predictable, a familiar face that's easily taken for granted, an old habit or hobby that comes back into our lives."[108]

My calling is to serve others through writing, coaching, and speaking. It's predictable. People who are closest to me know that I most likely have a journal or some writing tool with me at all times. I'm always taking notes and seeking lessons. I've been a coach long before I was being paid to do it. It's in me. I love helping others solve their problems or navigate their dreams.

Thankfully, we serve a patient God. He will guide us to what He has already placed in our hearts. Several years ago, I felt God tugging at my heart to move in a new direction. Sadly, I was too afraid to move forward. I didn't understand that if God were directing my steps, He would provide everything I needed to accomplish His will. Full of doubt, I questioned and avoided what I felt God was calling me to do. But God has taught me that if I believe His promises, He can do anything through me. Do you believe God's promises? How do we learn who God is and what He is capable of? Dive in! Read His Word. Go to church. Be the Church. Pray. "To be a Christian without prayer is no more possible than to be alive without breathing."[109]

Surround yourself with people seeking God's heart. Attend Christian conferences and read. If you're not a reader, listen to podcasts or audiobooks. I listen to podcasts while I'm getting dressed or traveling in the car for any length of time. I attend women's conferences, writers conferences, and leadership conferences. Through these experiences and your daily time with Him, God will reveal Himself. And, in reflection, you will be revealed. You'll begin to see who *you* are—who He created you to be. God is working in you as you learn more about who He is.

God wastes nothing! All of those jobs I took or distractions I created to avoid what I was called to do, God is using those. He is using my brokenness to help others heal from theirs. The butter tub may be empty, but it still has a purpose. It can again be useful. If you're feeling empty, know that God is ready and waiting to upcycle your emptiness into something you could never imagine. He is prepared to use all of your emptiness for His Kingdom's sake. Allow Him to use your pain. Leverage your pain to help other people. God wants us to be rivers, not reservoirs. Grandma's love still flows. She touched the lives of many people over her ninety-three years on earth, and now her legacy lives on in the ripple.

Kary Oberbrunner, in his book *The Deeper Path*, says, "We crave an illusion, a life without pain—but the price of such a life is one without love."[110] I can't imagine my life without Grandma's love. She helped shape me. Her legacy continues to stretch me and mold me into a woman of influence, following in her footsteps. Grief is the price of love. I'm honored to grieve because I was blessed with great love. Grandma's life well-lived served as the perfect example of what God is waiting to do through us. He wants to use what He has given us to bless those we meet. Allow His love to flow through your life, and your life will never end.

I'm still learning lessons as I reflect on the memories of Grandma, the influence she was in my life, and the impact she had on so many others. That's the beauty of a legacy that never ends. Some people think it's selfish to care about what people say after you're gone. I disagree! It isn't self-serving but serving others beyond your last breath. You'll never know—this side of heaven—the ripple effect your life will have, but you can do your best to make sure it's a ripple of love. In Ephesians, Paul reminds us, "As a prisoner for the Lord, then, I urge you to live a life worthy of the calling you have received."[111]

Grandma was thoughtful throughout her life. She left a legacy that will live on through many people. I consider it my highest honor to commemorate her life through this book and through my life's work.

In her writings, Grandma included these final paragraphs about her love for music. I guess she passed that on, as well. My uncle Joe was the lead singer in a band. We'd often go as a family to his dances. I first learned to dance at John T. Floore's Country Store in Helotes, Texas. When I was just a kid, my grandpa would let me step on his boots, and he'd scoot me around in a Texas Two-Step. Waltzing was always my favorite. It's such a proper dance and would make any girl feel like a princess, spinning around the dance floor. I taught my children how to dance at a young age, as well. We can tear up a dance floor! I still enjoy a night of dancing with the family. I have always loved music and dancing. Remember that boombox in the driveway? I create that experience often in my studio before I sit down to work. I crank up a worship song and just dance.

Grandma certainly passed on her love for music, even choosing such a meaningful song to be played at her memorial service.

Music has always been a pleasure to me. My father's family always enjoyed music. Many had bands in a small town south of Hallettsville, Texas. Before my dad died, he saw to it that my brother and I had lessons: me on the sax and Lawrence on violin. The first dance I ever attended, I played the sax in a band; my cousin, Anna Marie Ripps, played piano; brother Lawrence played violin; and the bandmaster's son played the drums. It was a country dance. I was nine years old.

We always had music on the radio. It didn't matter what station was on, I was happy with any music. All through life, when things got rough, music was soothing. In the last few years, I've learned through the local Public Broadcasting Station, KLRN, of Daniel O'Donnell. Many of the songs he composed himself. I've requested of my family one he wrote, "Beyond the Rainbow's End," be part of my memorial ceremony.[112] "Now all your thoughts of me, let them be joyful, of things we've done and happy times we've shared."[113]

I'm honored to grieve because I was blessed with great love.
#WorthSaving

Acknowledgements

From my humble heart, first and foremost, I thank my Lord and Savior Jesus Christ for giving me the gift of this opportunity, for the patience to see me through it, and for your unending guidance each step of the way.

To my husband, best friend, and supporter of every crazy dream—thank you. I love you! Thank you for allowing me the resources to research, write, and answer my calling. Thank you for loving me through the highs and lows of finding my way as a writer. Thank you for loving me as Christ loves the Church.

To Jenifer, my sister, my faithful research assistant, memory keeper, family historian, field-trip organizer, and cheerleader—I can't thank you enough. Without your encouragement, this may have never made it to print. I'm thankful to have you to share life with. I love you.

To my children—thank you for the lessons you've taught me. Thank you for every field trip you took with me to research for this and for never showing any doubt that this would one day happen. You inspire me! I truly love you so much it hurts.

To my mom—thank you for acknowledging me publicly as an author long before I was ready to acknowledge it myself. That day is a treasured memory! You made it a bit more real and a little less scary. I love you.

To my dear friend Melanie—thank you for encouraging me over the years and reminding me that I was designed for this. Thank you for your part in this project.

To my military buddy, Jennifer—thank you for shining my boots then and encouraging me now. It means more than you know.

To my Zoom ladies—thank you for holding my feet to the fire. Our time together has been sacred. I am blessed and honored to have you be a part of this journey.

To Barbara—thank you for your work with the photographs. I love that you treasure your family history as much as Jenifer and I do.

To my VIP Launch Team—thank you for celebrating with me each step of the way and for being a part of the ripple. Lives will be changed because of you!

To my editor, Dara—thank you for the finishing touches, the great feedback, and making me look like an author should.

To my mentor and coach, Kary—thank you for your obedience to the call on your life. Without you, I'd still be dreaming about this.

Endnotes

1   Warren, Rick. *The Purpose Driven Life.* Grand Rapids, Michigan: Zondervan, 2002.
2   Castro, Theresa. *The Dark Before the Dawn: 70 Secrets to Self-Discovery.* San Antonio, Texas: H and E Publishing, 2004.
3   Warren, *Purpose Driven,* 275.
4   Jeremiah 29:11
5   Centers for Disease Control and Prevention. "Lyme Disease." Accessed July 10, 2018. https://www.cdc.gov/lyme/treatment/.
6   "About BurningBoats.com." Accessed July 10, 2018. http://burningboats.com/about-burningboatscom/.
7   Pressfield, Steven. *Turning Pro.* New York: Black Irish Entertainment, 2012.
8   Warren, *Purpose Driven,* 275.
9   Isaiah 30:8.
10 Source unknown (quote credited to several different people).
11 Adlai E. Stevenson II.

12 2 Chronicles 7:14.
13 Alex Velarde of LifePoint Fellowship Church in Tyler, Texas.
14 *The Book of Eli.* Directed by the Hughes brothers. 2010. Warner Bros.
15 *Hoarders.* Executive producers Rob Sharenow, Jodi Flynn, Dave Severson, Matt Chan, Andrew Berg, Mike Kelly, Pat Barnes, and George Butts. 2009. A&E, Lifetime.
16 *American Idol.* Directed by Andy Scheer. 2002. FOX, ABC.
17 Hatmaker, Jen. *7: An Experimental Mutiny Against Excess.* (Nashville, Tennessee: B&H Publishing Group, 2012), 28.
18 Groeschel, Craig. *Leadership Podcast.*
19 Collins, Jim. "First Who—Get the Right People on the Bus." https://www.jimcollins.com/article_topics/articles/first-who.html.
20 Groeschel, Craig. April 7, 2016. "The Forbidden Phrase." Podcast audio. *Leadership Podcast.*
21 Psalm 37:4 ESV.
22 World Population Review. "San Antonio, Texas, Population 2018." worldpopulationreview.com/us-cities/san-antonio-population/.
23 Goff, Bob. *Love Does.* Nashville, Tennessee: Thomas Nelson, 2014.
24 John 5:6 NIV.
25 John 5:8 NIV.
26 Luke 23:34 ESV.
27 Proverbs 10:24.
28 James 4:17.
29 Velarde, Alex. April 29, 2018. "The Courage Gap." Podcast audio. *LifePoint Fellowship Church Podcast.*
30 Genesis 4:7.
31 Oberbrunner, Kary. Author Academy Elite, "How to Become an Author." bit.ly/AAEPublish.
32 *The Biggest Loser.* Executive producer Eden Gaha. 2008. NBC.

33 Point of Grace. "How You Live." *How You Live.* Word Records, 2007.

34 *For the Love of the Game.* Directed by Sam Raimi. 1999. Universal Pictures.

35 Buggy Barn Museum. "Who We Are." www.buggybarnmuseum.com.

36 United Nations Educational, Scientific and Cultural Organization (UNESCO). "World Heritage List." https://whc.unesco.org/en/list/.

37 Batterson, Mark. *Draw the Circle: The 40 Day Prayer Challenge.* Grand Rapids, Michigan: Zondervan, 2012.

38 Ecclesiastes 6:9.

39 Job 22:21–25.

40 New Life Foundation. "Welcome to Vernon Howard's Higher World." http://www.vernonhoward.com/.

41 Anton Ripps was Grandma's grandfather on her mother's side. He was married to Mary Woller Ripps and was a sheepherder on property he owned in Helotes, Texas. He died in 1937, when Grandma was fourteen years of age.

42 Romans 10:9.

43 Mariah Carey. "Hero." *Music Box.* Columbia Records,1993.

44 Luke 17: 20–21.

45 Galatians 5:22.

46 Galatians 5:24–25.

47 Genesis 22: 1-18.

48 Matthew 6:26.

49 Luke 3:11.

50 TOMS Shoes. "Improving Lives." https://www.toms.com/improving-lives.

51 Church Under A Bridge. "A Family of Believers." https://cuabtyler.org/.

52 Warrior and Family Support Center, San Antonio, Texas. https://www.facebook.com/WarriorFamilySupportCenter/.

53 Matthew 26:5.

54 Matthew 6:27.

55 Genesis 37:19.

56 Romans 8:28.

57 Hostess of *Wheel of Fortune,* 1982–present.

58 Foster, Jim. *The Brownsville Herald.* "May/3 otdrs. Walt Makes Mark at Bait Stand, on Bar," Last modified May 3, 1998. Accessed July 5, 2018. https://www.brownsvilleherald.com/news/local/may-otdrs-walt-makes-mark-at-bait-stand-on-bar/article_455ba26c-b3ba-5e8f-8f1b-b7d8b5c375aa.html.

59 Ephesians 5:25.

60 Community Bible Church. www.communitybible.com.

61 Matthew 6:21.

62 Dexter Godfrey, speaker: Igniting Souls Conference 2017. http://bit.ly/BestConference4Creatives.

63 Appelt's Hill Gun Club. "About Us." https://appelthill-gunclub.com/about-us.

64 *Dance Hall Days.* Directed by Erik McCowan. 2018. https://www.dancehallroadtrip.com/dancehalldays.

65 *What Not To Wear.* Presented by Stacy London, Wayne Scot Lukas (season 1), Clinton Kelly (season 2–10). 2003. TLC.

66 James 2:26.

67 MissionLab. "MISSIONLAB: Learn Missions. Do Missions. Be a Missionary." http://www.missionlab.com/.

68 Amazon Outreach. http://amazonoutreach.org/.

69 Mathew 5:13.

70 YWAM. "Youth With A Mission Worldwide." https://www.ywam.org/.

71 Joshua 4:6–7.

72 Isaiah 43:15–19.

73 Psalm 9:1.

74 2 Timothy 1:7 ESV.

75 Romans 8:37.

76 Slater, Lyn. "Accidental Icon." https://www.accidentalicon.com/.

77 Batterson. *Draw the Circle.*

78 Addison Road. "Hope Now." *Hope Now.* Produced by Christopher Stevens INO Records, 2008.

79 Chandler, Matt. "Ecclesiastes—Part 9: Coffee with Granddaddy Part 1." Sermon, The Village Church, Flower Mound, TX, September 17, 2006. https://d1nw-frzxhi18dp.cloudfront.net/uploads/resource_library/attachment/file/825/200609170900HVWC21ASAAA_MattChandler_EcclesiastesPt9-CoffeeWithGranddaddyPt1.pdf.

80 The Village Church. https://www.thevillagechurch.net.

81 Proverbs 18:21 MSG.

82 Exodus 14:16 ESV.

83 Oberbrunner. Author Academy Elite. bit.ly/AAEPublish.

84 Dexter Godfrey, speaker: Igniting Souls Conference 2017. http://bit.ly/BestConference4Creatives.

85 Ephesians 4:17.

86 Owned by the Quiñones Family since 1949. http://www.jacala.com.

87 Philippians 3:13.

88 Aitchison, Steven. Twitter post. May 18, 2015, 9:57 p.m. https://twitter.com/StevenAitchison/status/600480289773727744.

89 Goins, Jeff. *The Art of Work: A Proven Path to Discovering What You Were Meant to Do* (Nashville, Tennessee: Thomas Nelson, 2015), 18.

90 West, Matthew. "Do Something." *Into the Light.* Produced by Pete Kipley. Sparrow Records, 2012.

91 Oberbrunner. Author Academy Elite. bit.ly/AAEPublish.

92 *Survivor.* Presented by Jeff Probst. 2000. CBS.

93 John 8:12 ESV.

94 *Shrek.* Directed by Andrew Adamson and Vicky Jenson. 2001. DreamWorks Pictures.

95 Psalm 37:4.

96 Mark 12:31.

97 Proverbs 9:11.

98   Turley, Joan L. *Sacred Work in Secular Places.* Powell, Ohio: Author Academy Elite, 2017. bit.ly/AAEPublish.

99   Now called "Diocese of Orange Christ Cathedral." https://christcathedralcalifornia.org/.

100   Matthew 5:14–16.

101   Cole, Nat King. "Nature Boy." *Mona Lisa.* Capitol Records, 1950.

102   John 13:35.

103   1Corinthians 13:4–8.

104   Maxwell, John C. *The Leadership Handbook: 26 Critical Lessons Every Leader Needs* (Nashville, Tennessee: Thomas Nelson, 2015), 244.

105   Theodore Geisel, better known as Dr. Seuss.

106   Found this credited to Thomas S. Monson, 16th president of the Church of Jesus Christ of Latter-day Saints (2008–2018).

107   Brian J. Dixon, speaker: Igniting Souls Conference 2017. http://bit.ly/BestConference4Creatives.

108   Goins. *The Art of Work*, 170.

109   Martin Luther.

110   Oberbrunner, Kary. *The Deeper Path: Five Steps That Let Your Hurts Lead to Your Healing,* (Powell, Ohio: Author Academy Elite, 2018). bit.ly/AAEPublish.

111   Ephesians 4:1 NIV.

112   Grandma wrote the full lyrics in her notebook. What a sweet gift!

113   O'Donnell, Daniel. "Rainbow's End." *Until The Next Time.* DPTV Media, 2006.

Note from the Author

Usually, this spot is reserved for telling you, in third person, how great I am. Well, I don't like boring author bios, so I thought I'd just write from my heart.

My name is Brenda, and I'm a cry baby. I mean, if you spend enough time around me, you will probably see me cry. Seeing others cry makes me cry. Tears of joy or sadness, they flow just the same. I'm a romantic sap. I love LOVE!

I spent many years not feeling loved and wondering about my own worth. Now I help others discover their worth. Through my transparency, I help individuals move along their faith journey. **It is a journey!**

I've been sharing transformative messages since 2006. Through my writing, coaching, and speaking, I seek to serve the defeated, discouraged, and distracted. I want you to live a life worthy of your calling. I value life experience, relationships, creativity, and continual learning.

I love to do the unexpected. I've completed four half marathons and a sprint triathlon just to prove I could. I currently serve our community as the Director of LifeGroups and Social Media Content at our church.

My hubs (as I so lovingly refer to him on social media), Darren, and I are both military veterans. We love hiking and chasing waterfalls. We live in Texas with our beautifully blended family: Brittany, her husband Jake, and my adorable grandson Hayes; James and his wife Rachel; Beth (please wait about five more years to get married); and our loyal Jack Russell, Maggie.

Connect with other
Save the Butter Tubs!
fans or share your favorite
thoughts from the book using
#WorthSaving.

*Brenda also left you quotes at
the end of each chapter to share
across your social media.*

Don't forget to share
your victories using
#CelebrateToReplicate!

Take Your Next Step

It's your turn! It's time to trash the lies, treasure the truths, and transform your life and legacy!

You don't have to do this alone! Imagine Brenda leading you through a transformational process, in which you will discover your worth and purpose in a whole new way!

Open to participants around the world!

A focused, fearless, and fulfilling life is waiting for you! Take the next step at BrendaHaire.com.

What's the cost of staying defeated, discouraged, and distracted?

Bring Brenda into
Your Organization or Business

Speaker. Coach. Author. Torchbearer. Trainer.

Brenda's transparency will immediately connect her to the hearts of your audience. Whether it's a keynote or a workshop, she will customize her message and training to achieve a life-changing impact. Brenda knows the importance of finding the right speaker for your event and setting the tone for transformation to take place.

**Contact Brenda Today
to Begin the Conversation.
BrendaHaire.com**